Gnosis and the Theocrats
from Mars

Illuminating Modernity

Illuminating Modernity is dedicated to the renewal of faith in a world that is both Godless and idolatrous. This renewal takes the legacy of faith seriously and explores the tradition in the hope that the means of its contemporary development are to be found within it. This approach takes the historical crisis of faith seriously and makes sincere efforts to receive the strength necessary for a renewal. We call our way the Franciscan option. And yet, one of the greatest resources upon which we hope to build is Thomism, especially those hidden treasures of modern Thomistic thought to be found in Continental and phenomenological philosophy and theology.

The Franciscan option takes the history of faith seriously both in its continuity and in its change. It takes seriously the tragic experiences of the history of faith since the Wars of Religion and especially in late modernity. But it also takes seriously the rich heritage of faith As Michael Polanyi argued, faith has become the fundamental act of human persons. Faith involves the whole of the person in his or her absolute openness to the Absolute. As Hegel saw, the logic of history is prefigured in the story of the Gospels, and the great and transforming experience of humanity has remained the experience of resurrection in the aftermath of a dramatic death.

The series editors are boundlessly grateful to Anna Turton, whose support for this series made a hope into a reality. We also owe a huge debt of gratitude to Notre Dame's Nanovic Institute for European Studies for giving us financial and moral support at the outset of our project. Many thanks to Anthony Monta and James McAdams for caring about the "Hidden Treasures."

Gnosis and the Theocrats from Mars

Francesca Aran Murphy

LONDON • NEW YORK • OXFORD • NEW DELHI • SYDNEY

T&T CLARK

Bloomsbury Publishing Plc

50 Bedford Square, London, WC1B 3DP, UK
1385 Broadway, New York, NY 10018, USA
29 Earlsfort Terrace, Dublin 2, Ireland

BLOOMSBURY, T&T CLARK and the T&T Clark logo are trademarks of
Bloomsbury Publishing Plc

First published in Great Britain 2020
This edition published in 2022

Copyright © Francesca Aran Murphy, 2020

Francesca Aran Murphy has asserted her right under the Copyright, Designs and
Patents Act, 1988, to be identified as Author of this work.

For legal purposes the Acknowledgments on p. viii constitute an
extension of this copyright page.

Cover design: Terry Woodley
Cover image: *The Ascension of Christ*, by Andrea Mantegna
(1431–1506) © Leemage/Getty

All rights reserved. No part of this publication may be reproduced or
transmitted in any form or by any means, electronic or mechanical,
including photocopying, recording, or any information storage or retrieval
system, without prior permission in writing from the publishers.

Bloomsbury Publishing Plc does not have any control over, or responsibility for,
any third-party websites referred to or in this book. All internet addresses given
in this book were correct at the time of going to press. The author and publisher
regret any inconvenience caused if addresses have changed or sites have ceased
to exist, but can accept no responsibility for any such changes.

A catalogue record for this book is available from the British Library.

A catalog record for this book is available from the Library of Congress.

ISBN: HB: 978-0-5676-8051-8
PB: 978-0-5676-9698-4
ePDF: 978-0-5676-8052-5
eBook: 978-0-5676-8055-6

Series: Illuminating Modernity

Typeset by Integra Software Services Pvt. Ltd.

To find out more about our authors and books visit www.bloomsbury.com
and sign up for our newsletters.

This book is dedicated to Ken and Balázs, who know that "only a god can save us now."

Contents

Acknowledgments — viii

1 Beneficiaries of the Theocracy — 1
2 Unlike Human Beings — 5
3 Deus Ex Machina — 13
4 A Brief History of Pre-Theocratic Times — 23
5 Routine Times — 39
6 The Secular Sanctity of Lacordaire — 47
7 Soulless Angels and Pirates — 55
8 A Trail of Elephants — 61
9 An Absence of Volition — 67
10 Secularity versus Secularization — 73
11 The Trojan Horse: Comedy Regained — 79
12 Kidnapped! — 89
13 What Is Slavery? — 93
14 The Bodhissatva Henri-Dominique Lacordaire — 107
15 The New Prometheus — 113
Envoi — 121

Bibliography — 122
Index — 123

Acknowledgments

I would like to thank the Templeton Foundation, which, through the good offices of Rusty Reno, funded the year-long sabbatical which enabled this project. I would also like to thank the Issachar Fund who co-funded this sabbatical year. Tis novel could not have been written without the support of the Templeton Foundation and the Issachar Fund.

The original text of this book was given as The Pentecost Lectures at Pluscarden Abbey, Scotland, in 2017. I am very grateful to the monks of the abbey for their hospitality.

Disclaimer

This is a work of fiction and any resemblance of any of the characters to any living person is a fluke, and not the design of the author.

1

Beneficiaries of the Theocracy

The Theocrats arrived on a clear, blue September day. Every native New Yorker who saw their fleet breaching the unclouded Manhattan sky remembered their first sight of the heavenly host. Every native New Yorker looked up and said, in Mandarin, Portuguese, Urdu, Spanish, Yoruba, or Parsi, "only in New York." All of the Pentecostals said the same in the ancient Brooklynese tongue, which abruptly but briefly became a living language. The event was facebooked before it actually happened, due to the Theocrats' way of turning time into space. Their morphing way with time permitted them to materialize before their ships entered American airspace. The Theocrats were expert at anticipating thought with images, so the landing was on TV before anyone knew it happened. Many on the Arab street cheered, thinking it meant the end for Western Crusaders. People glued to their screens around the world hoped that the evidently opulent Theocrats came bearing solutions to the galloping Riders of war, famine, disease, and fatalism. Many believed fervently that an intergalactic task force could simultaneously call a halt to globalization and let the nations breathe as one. The optimists cheered in anticipation of world peace and plenty. Surely these guys who had punctured the skies in their space ships could roll back the ozone layers and turn the tide of global warming. Even the pessimists opined that the aeronauts brought fortune and happiness. Since all humanity desires happiness, optimist and pessimist alike throughout Africa, Russia, and Asia cheered on the invasion of America by glassy Theocratic robots. They cheered in unison with most Americans who could see that the Martians came bearing many gifts. Everyone had a story to tell about that day, and not one of the stories raised a smile.

The Theocrats did not bring happiness, or even humor. It is mind-boggling to consider listing the things people stopped seeing the funny side of during Earth's Theocratic Epoch. The role of comedienne was endangered, as was Rom-Com writer, stand-up, slapstick double, and even clown. Pistis, our heroine, was for long denied the vocation for which she was best suited. But it was Gnosis 777, the guy she would have hated at the start and then married forever, who often complained, *why can't I tell a joke? what's gagging me? who is autocorrecting my wit? where's the laughs?*

Human beings quickly learned to see themselves as BOTTs, or Beneficiaries of the Theocracy. They learned to call their Earth Oz, as their benefactors did. The satellites of glassy gray which ceaselessly circulated the New Oz, threw all of it into a serious light. The sunshine itself was painted gray by ubiquitous glass. The cinereal taup killed the need to wear shades, so sunglasses too went the way of Reese Witherspoon. The all-pervading irenicism of the Martians was so incontestably high-minded that it took staunch piety or downright cynicism to doubt that the invasion was what the Robots said it was. Once upon a time, both Cult and Gnosis had been Hoaxers. As one who lent to credulity, Cult had initially believed that numerous inter-governmental agencies were conspiring to pretend the earth had been taken over by Martians; as a dyed in the wool sceptic, Gnosis struggled to disavow the notion that they were being sold. It was the incessant gray light which finally persuaded the Hoaxers that the invasion was neither an advertising gimmick or government propaganda, nor a virtual game, nor a feint. They were not being played. The conquest was happening in real life, in real time and space.

Rather than enriching humanity with comedy, the Theocrats dispelled its demons. Upon making their autumnal touch down, they immediately hurled their computational spells against viruses and cast out climate change. They cast it out so thoroughly that the climate and even the weather itself scarcely changed again, from one season to the next. A changeling season of incessant good will commenced. The Robots from Mars brought peace, plenty, and good fortune for every person alive that day. World hunger was soon forgotten like a bad dream from long ago. They flattened the Pope and gave the wealth of the Vatican to the poor, who needed it more. The promise of the Theocrats was war no more, and they made good on it. They brought the gift of peace and who could argue with that?

The invaders did not come from outside of time, but they moved so fast that temporality bowed before them. They did not so much inhabit past, present, or future as bend the times directly to their will. It was a foregone conclusion that most people on earth would surrender their freedoms to the Theocrats because they were not given time to think it through. The conquest happened too fast. "He who hesitates is lost," was never truer than on that September day. Most human thought is hesitant, roundabout, or at best discursive. To top it off, the gift the Martians brought seemed so good that it just had to be true.

It was hard not to feel sentiments of reverence for these veritable harbingers of a modestly secular kingdom of God. The new regnant lords of Oz did not insist upon it. They were not jealous gods. The Theocrats gave their blessing to a multitude of religions. All they asked of the BOTTs was the weekly ignition of a scented candle. Cult 665 bought his in a store which exhorted its customers to "be the change you want": "buy the change you lack," Gnosis would have snorted, if he could have permitted himself a joke. The candles were set outside people's doors, or on the porch; people who lived in apartment blocks set them in windows or on their balcony.

2

Unlike Human Beings

Gnosis leaned into the bar and called to the bartender, "Cult, where's the remote?" It was an impolite reminder that the TVs should turn to the news channel in time for the regulars' nightly fare of long-distance misery pornography. The distance was light years. The drinkers stared at the five foot flat screens to enjoy scenes of plague, starvation, and civil war in galaxies too far away to benefit from Theocratic conquest. Now that Earth life was lacking in suspense, let alone true drama, aspiration to playing the hero had been replaced by addiction to images of spectacular beauty. The Cult regulars were nightly transfixed by images of mutilated, suffocating, and famine-wrenched faces, faces which slaked their hearts' repressed lust to do good by making them feel good. Cult and Gnosis sipped their beers meditatively and drank in the dehydrated bodies and limbs of the denizens of a distant star which had succumbed to drought before the Theocrats could secularize it. Images of egregious poverty magnetized every eye in the bar. "Theocracy sure beats dying of thirst," said Cult. Few of the regulars unglued their eyes long enough to nod assent to this self-evident proposition. Gnosis could not resist clicking on what felt to him, alone, like bait. "How come we call the Martians Theocrats when they are not religious?" he asked an audience whose attention was fixed elsewhere. One person was listening. But it was Cult who answered, loftily, "The Martians say God is beyond all the religions. That's what makes the Theocracy the first and only religion of peace." "Except for that it's not a religion," someone mumbled into his beer, "it's not closed minded." Cult readily corrected himself, agreeing that the Theocrats were peace-bearers, not a religion of peace as such! "So it's not weird that the Theocracy is indistinguishable from global atheism?" Gnosis inquired.

It was not a rhetorical question to him. Gnosis had no rhetorical questions, only *how come?* and *why?* Gnosis needed to know. He wanted to know more than he wanted any other thing. The moment of truth, the vivid act of mental illumination, was his happiness. Like most other wise-guys, he wished he could board the Robot ships and find out how they worked; along with the rest of his breed, he dreamed of taking a Robot apart and re-assembling it, to find out what made it tick. This aspiration being barred to him, he could only feed on abstract hypotheses and speculations about the Robotic modus operandi. This is why he wondered aloud, on this charcoal gray evening, how this compound of secularizing and theocracy building held together.

Cult went back to pouring drinks for his screen-rapt customers. The Theocracy had terminated world hunger, and brought the climate to heel. The Robots had answered all the problems of the human race to the last decimal point. They had ended war forever, by neutralizing the appetites which lived so dangerously close to the fighting-urge, like the appetite for imposing one's own religion on one's neighbors—whatever that religion might be. They had given the world's former leaders the gifts which they had promised them in return for world leadership. Their problems solved by the square-root of minus one, it was a rare BOTT who gave a rats' arse how come every human question had been secularized under the Theocracy. They were free to inquire about anything on the fixed menu the Robots had given them.

They were free to apply to wear the electronic collars, but only a select few were permitted to do so. The collars emitted a light electronic shock at apparently random intervals, whenever the owners decided to tap them. It was an experiential testimony of the deep and profound mystery which underpinned the Robots' integral mechanical predicability. On the day after the Landing, folks had lined up for the implantation ceremony. The implantation machines that were set up in public squares were like guillotines, neatly dividing head from body. The collars were an external symbol of devout submission to the *One,* the Robot Theocracy. No matter how well the wearers of this prized status symbol knew that they had not committed the least crime in thought, word, or deed, still the shocks occasioned deep feelings of guilt, remorse, and self-reflection. The indecipherable and punitive messages came to be regarded as a kind of moral GPS, and the wearers were not only celebrities, but were spontaneously accorded moral leadership. How could they know that the Robots had chosen these heroes on the basis of their strong bladder control? The collar-wearers were said to live entirely in their thoughts, to have achieved the dream of Descartes, and to be virtually cognition machines. They would not dream of questioning the Theocracy.

So Pistis was truly the only one there who could hear the questions Gnosis 777 asked. The bottled comedienne rashly inquired, "Are you a believer yourself? Are you religious?" "Hell I'm not," Gnosis snorted. With the boisterous makeup of a bar-tender, Cult could not resist pursuing an interrogation. "Are you a speciesist? Do you think humans matter more than Robots?" "Nope." "Are you Earth-centrist? Nostalgic for the Age of Faith?" blustered the bartender. "No, I'm down with Galileo," said Gnosis sarcastically. Cult pursued his mock bumptious questioning for the fun of it: "Why does it matter that the Theocrats are secularists any more than that they are Martians or Robots?" Gnosis paused. "It's a contradiction in terms," he said slowly. "How can secularists be Theocrats?"

Cult was not a curious man. He said complacently and with persuasive certainty that Robots are lots of things, but not religious. How could a Robot be religious? Can you imagine one going to Church or praying or *lighting a candle* to its god? Impossible! The Theocratic government was not odds with the secularism it imposed because it wasn't a *religious* Theocracy. Everyone around the bar assented to that plausible proposition. Contradictions do not exist; it is impossible for some one thing simultaneously to be the opposite of itself. So it could not be a contradiction that the Robots had ruled theocratically and had thereby achieved a near-planetary secularization.

Pistis's uncle had warned her many times against public displays of nonconformity. The Robots did not need to do much censoring, because human fear of breaking taboos did much of that work for them. So long as the BOTTs did not attempt to avoid surveillance, their movements were not much restricted; their converse was only monitored sporadically. Nonetheless, it was dangerous to be a known public rebel. Cult's anti-intellectual pietism made Pistis see red, the law of non-contradiction enraged her Parisian soul, and when she saw she had all the drinkers around the bar against her, she lost her cool. The fact that she could not articulate what made the Robot Conquerors of time and space into Theocrats was no obstacle but a spur to her entrance into a debate with strangers in a bar. Sitting on her hands to keep them from shaking, she asserted, "Perhaps it's more a paradox than a contradiction." "What's the difference?" Cult replied, though he was not asking.

Pistis was smart enough not to lecture them on paradox. She tried another tack. "Secularism is a thing. It's a thing like religion when it expands and fills the horizon." Gnosis tried to translate her lyrical cogitations into rational thought. "You're saying it tries to monopolize the market." Pistis assented, saying, "The only way to prove secularism has all the right answers is to require that it has the only right questions." Cult figured, "The market still decides!" "No," Pistis observed mildly. "Secularism doesn't sell itself as one thing we can buy into or not. It doesn't ask us to consent and buy, it asks for commitment. That's like religion. Secularism is Religion-like."

Gnosis was intrigued but not persuaded. He didn't see his way to equating two opposite systems like theocracy and secularism just because they share universalism and belief that the truth of their system was beyond discussion. He could not swallow the absurdity of saying that one thing which walks like a duck and quacks like a duck was one and the same as another thing which walks and talks like a duck shooting hill billy. Gnosis enjoyed absurdity, deep down. But his rational mind would never concede that. He knew what the Ayatollahs looked like, back in the day when they ruled the roost in the desert, and he knew the figure the Martian Robots cut. It didn't compute to say they were one and the same. The Martians were no Mullahs: they had hunted the recidivists down and vaporized them to dust. The outlines of faces and hands of the last human theocrats were etched on the pavements of Mecca, where they had gathered for their last stand. Gnosis remembered the chalky silhouettes into which the Martians had vaped the Mullahs, and insisted, "No, that's not a religion-like thing!"

Almost no-one else, amongst the semi-secularized or casually spiritual earthlings who had watched open-mouthed as the Theocrats descended to the 9/11 Memorial in downtown Manhattan, cared two whits whether it was a contradiction or a paradox that their conquerors were both Theocrat and secularist. But Pistis, here, a true believer, in some one religion, observed that the Robots, too, were true believers and authentic Theocrats, not despite their godlessness, not bypassing their vaporizing of God and the gods, but in and through their glacial secularity. Cult could see the pair had a long future ahead in his bar, and jovially poured them both another icy drink.

Pistis asked, "Would you say the Theocrats are humanists?" Gnosis suppressed the image of screaming bearded men turning into flakes of ash. Cult said, "All humans are BOTTs now." "So yes?" Pistis asked Gnosis, looking him straight in the eye. "They want every BOTT on Oz to fulfill his or her own dreams," said Cultic. The same scruple which prevented Gnosis from calling a secularist-Mullah-eliminator a "Theocrat" debarred him from ascribing integral humanism to robotic Things from Mars. "They care for humanity," Cult insisted, "what else do you call humanism?" To him it seemed clear that the Robots were philanthropists, lovers of the "anthropos," of humanity. The Martians were the telescopic philanthropists of the time when science fiction took flesh, and consumed it.

"They descended from the skies like gods," mused Cult, his literal-mindedness coming inadvertently to Pistis's rescue. "That's right," she said, "they came from up above and they live up there in their satellite Olympiads." "They position themselves as gods," Gnosis conceded. "But what does it matter where they are?" "What do you think follows?" asked Pistis rather than putting words into his mouth. The three reflected on the all-powerful Olympic satellites from which Oz was governed. "They've decided to take the place of gods, unseat them, usurp them, whatever," Gnosis replied. "And so their secularism is our religion," said Pistis. "Ye shall be as gods," quothe the bartender, explaining airily, "I think Abraham Lincoln said that."

"They don't care about God. They care about humanity," Gnosis objected. Pistis disagreed, saying, "You cannot care for humanity from outside of it." She flashed him a look, and they shared the tacit thought that Robots are about as outside of humanity as one can be. "The Theocrats watch over the earth like tourists at the Aquatic zoo." "There's a glass wall between us," Gnosis admitted. And now, incautiously forgoing tacit hints, she insisted, "What they care about is being godlike, not about humanity!" They watched as the Robots whirred by high above, wheeling like whirring ferris-wheels, with one great eye at the center, and multiple eyes on each of their rotating cars. Everyone in the bar paused to hear the Robots sing "Eye, Eye," as they spun. "The Watchers," said Cult piously. "Their thing is surveillance, and watching is what they do," said Gnosis, not agreeing or disagreeing with Pistis. He was not sure where this was going. He tried to stay sober and concentrate. "The Martians see straight through our human experience. It counts for nothing. It makes no odds to them what things look like for us," she told him: "They take a god-like view of us, and our problems, and they fix things for us, externally, not from inside." The glassy-eyed Robots saw through everything in the unblinking of their Eye. "That makes them pretend gods and it makes for a simulated theocracy not a real one," said Gnosis, in whom the habits of the skeptical Hoaxer died hard. The time-morphing Martians were not enough of an anthropomorphic projection to make the cut as Deities.

Gnosis and Pistis went home in agreement in this at least, that Oz was ruled by a religion-like thing. Their secularist benefactors were masters of illusion, and the Theocracy was perhaps the greatest mirage of all. There was nothing supernatural about them, that was for sure, but our mere human nature was a small thing in their glassy eyes. They scanned the human condition from outside and above it, and seemed therefore to transcend it.

Cult headed upstairs to light his candle to the Theocrats. Pistis lit a candle too, when she got back to her apartment, before the statue of a saint whom a shady antique dealer had assured her was Henri-Dominique Lacordaire. Pistis's credulity was to a different power than Cult's. She had decorated the base of the statue with the Dominican's own words, "J'espère mourir en religieus pénitent eten libéral impénitent." The nineteenth-century French champion of secularity and freedom has never been canonized, so the antique dealer was probably economical with the truth. "The rights of God are the rights of humanity," Pistis murmured, as she invoked the Dominican Boddhisatva, patron "saint" of freedom for God and for man. Gnosis watched sports on TV for hours, sleeplessly wondering how secularization could spell theocracy. The trio venerated their gods.

3

Deus Ex Machina

Gnosis had a sleepless night. Meditating on the world's rotating Rulers made his mind whirl. He didn't want to do anything that would trigger the solicitude of the Robots, so he tried to lay rigidly still. The more he struggled to immobilize himself, the more he thrashed. He used his left side, he used his right, he slumped backward, he tried going full fetal, then he stretched out flat on his face. He balled up his pillow under his head and then threw it out of the bed. He kept arguing with a phantom image of Pistis, explaining how unconvinced he was by her reasons the Robots have become our gods. But even his made-up phantom image of Pistis just kept smiling and shaking her head. He could not get his own imaginary woman to buy his counter-arguments. The stubborn girl would be one of the hold outs, the querulous Pistocenes. Why do Christian heresies have such weird names, Gnosis asked himself, feeling grateful to take his file name and number from the Martian folder on BOTT philosophies. And a skeptical philosophy at that he thought proudly. But his pride dissolved again into irritation, since his phantom woman was not only mute but deaf as well!

There was a danger that the Robots would eye out a BOTT in discomfort, and come, like attentive medics, to inventory what was broken and fix it. If Gnosis could not stop fidgeting, he would wake upon a moving walkway into the Sleeping Room. The Robots used the Room to store insomniac BOTTs while they were working on them. Rebotting them! The Sleeping Room had the fuel smell of the auto-repair shop and it played its part in mechanizing the soul's operations, checking the tires and replacing the oil of gladness with less flammable ungents. Gnosis knew the peril in which his gyrations were placing him. The Robots had weapons which turned rebels into ashes for their own peace of mind, and so too they had radiopathic surgeries which would send a guy to sleep, or make him forget his grief, and which washed bad memories right out of a girl's hair. Gnosis knew he had to stay off that conveyor belt if he wanted ever to know why this invasion had spawned religious veneration for the conquerors. If the Robots' sensors picked up on the pain of his questioning, they would silence his internal dialogues, erasing his unheeded hectoring of an imagined Pistis. So he wrapped his ankles around themselves, locked his arms round his chest, and compelled himself to lie like a board.

He tried to run point by point through everything Pistis had said and figure out why he could not buy each item. She seemed at first to say that human beings had substituted the Robots for God. When it started out, her argument seemed to be that humans had made the Robots the be all and end all of their lives. The Robots were the Tops for humans, and so they were our gods? Was that what she had said? Gnosis just could not believe that *whatever* is the Tops for a guy is his God. "Baseball is not my god," he informed his absentee audience of one, "and I don't worship the Oriols." To believe that whatever is Tops for a person is their God, one would have to classify whatever they like doing best as worship. Watching sports didn't give Gnosis any churchy worshipful feeling. He just liked it. Back in the day, when BOTTs were permitted their own vehicles, his friends who fancied themselves as amateur mechanics did not worship their cars. Only some pious preacher would call cars a god-substitute. Gnosis was not persuaded by the sermony idea that what he loved best was God to him. If they wanted to prove that his love for baseball was idolatry, the believers would have to start by convincing him that what he was looking for in baseball is not just *sports* but *god almighty*.

Gnosis reflected that Pistis had said nothing to persuade him that there is a true god. She had tried instead to get him picturing the Robots, their benefactors, as false gods. The stubborn woman had said that the Robots were false gods because they were too inhuman. What a weird claim for a believer to make, Gnosis thought, gripping his T-shirt with his fingers to stop himself running his hands through his hair. Weren't believers supposed to fight the theory that God is just a projection of ourselves? He momentarily forgot that she had coaxed *him* into calling the Robots pretend gods, and then, he remembered that he'd walked right into a booby trap there! An elephant trap, Gnosis snickered, picturing the elephantine icons which encircled the globe. He had fallen for it because it had sparked that nerve in him that wondered if all this Philanthropy was a swindle and the Martians con-men of a higher order. He would have sat up and slapped himself on the head if he had not suddenly glimpsed the radiating bulbs, observing him with diagnostic curiosity, concerned only for his well-being. It was bad news when the lights started flashing.

Concerned only for his happiness. Gnosis said to the annoying woman who did not lie beside him, '*au contraire,* Pistis 475, those Robots are more like *we want God to be than any deity the human race has ever worshiped.* They've given us what we have always sought from the gods! They hand over what all the old gods refused to give! They've solved all the problems of the human race! No more praying to a deity who might not come through! The prayers of believers used to be answered just often enough for them to be disappointed when their gods held out on them. That time was so over now. No more fearing Jehovah's wrath for an offence you didn't know you commit. No shouting out Allahu Akbar right before the incinerators mashed you to pulp. No more madcap prophets dancing around their capricious gods. No more good luck today, rendezvous with the Grim Reaper tomorrow. No more dervishes because no more whimsical Despot Deity. No more fiery mystery! You could, Gnosis figured, calculate exactly how long it would take for the Robots to swoop in on him and rescue him from sleeplessly playing the prosecutor in an internal court room drama. Once they saw a BOTT had a problem, they were *on it*. No God the human race had ever worshiped had been as god-like as this, Gnosis gamely asserted to his fantasy audience. Forget stubborn Pistis's "your highest good is your God" pieties! The Robots were as good as they were all powerful, and they were not scary or unpredictable.

He had just enough time to snort to himself, "the Robots don't *punish* us for being human" when all the lights flipped on in his apartment. Two Robot medics slide through the porous gel walls with which they had dignified every BOTT abode. The physical gyrations that accompanied Gnosis's mental to-and-fro had been recorded by benign cameras, and he was fortunate merely to ignite an orange alert in their fortuity-detectors. Random and fortuitous events must be brought back into pattern-formation, to prevent the Robots' charges from self-harm. Long ago, the Martian machines had been programmed to serve by their designers, and even their overthrow of those celestial Roboticists had been an act of kindness. The servant-kings of Oz had espied that Gnosis was in need of their help, and their benefactions were inescapable.

"Hi guys!" he said ineffectually to the two sleep-policing machines, as their sensory rods and scanning staffs troubleshot his brain waves. They were looking to quantify his dysfunction. If Gnosis 777 was repairable, their radiopathic rays would reboot him and retool him. They looked into every angle for repair before they painlessly eliminated a BOTT's animation functions and harvested its hardware. Gnosis knew his life was in the hands of mechanics who viewed his consciousness as the interaction of hard drives and software. He knew he was in peril of the path from the Sleeping Room to the Recycling Machine. He explained that he was not sleepless, just itchy.

He had indeed been scratching a mental itch, so his story did not trigger the Martian lie-detectors. Gnosis had through many an encounter with Robots become practically Jesuitical in his use of casuistry. The affectless machines could seldom detect half-lies and half-truths. Nothing springing from the realm of the imagination or emotions fell under their radar. Though they could beat the BOTTs at every game, they were too humorless to know when they were being played. They had the Intel on the multiple meanings of individual words, but their supermassive brains could scarcely process a casual, conversational use of verbal analogy.

"I was thinking about a beautiful woman," Gnosis told the sleep-policing duo in all truthfulness. He thought of tossing in, "discussing theodicy," but the Robots were impervious to satire. So he walled his teeth against sarcasm. "Masturbating?" they asked tonelessly, as their eyes blankly surveyed his brain. "Mental masturbation," Gnosis replied, betting his life on their inability to compute a metaphor. He had to be truthful, but what is truth? For the theocratic Brain-Boxes, truth was the adequacy of the data and the facts. Configuring information and facts was the full extent their lie detecting ran. Once, in the early days before BOTT driving was outlawed, Gnosis had escaped death by speeding ticket by telling a Robotic traffic-cop he had been meditating on Being. The gamble paid off again tonight. "Too much of that makes you go blind," said one of the officers with a mock finger wag, displaying the Theocrat humor at its most hilarious. Gnosis kept up his rictus grin until long after the sleep-cops had marched out and rotated away to the skies, singing tunelessly as they flew, "Eye for Eye."

"You could not make this stuff up," Gnosis said to himself as he slipped under the duvet and froze in the posture of one deep in relaxing sleep. The man of constant questions was sure of just one thing that the Robots had come at a providential time. They had arrived when their moment was awaited, like Spring when a dreary March slips into cool April. They had come to divest us of the liberties with which we harm and trouble ourselves at the fateful juncture when most people were ready to call it a day. The great inventions were achieved when people had felt a tacit need for them, our outward culture fitting the inward desires of humanity like a skin. The Robots had likewise put us under their omnipotent protectorate at a time when freedom was too great a risk to bear. The time was ripe for the Robots to conduct a mechanical rescue of humanity from itself. The conquest effected a transition so seamless that it felt like the next step, and had none of the appearance of a dystopia in a movie or a novel. It was time for a medical intervention and human beings wanted nothing more than to be the patient. They competed to wear the collars which simultaneously enculpated them for nameless crimes and numbed their free spirits.

Gnosis had always thought that was strange, because he fancied that it was in the time of the clerical power and religious superstition that freedom was discounted. But Gnosis was weary, now, and slowly but surely repressed the stream of questions about why human liberties had so easily been traded in for lifelong security. Why had the *Muslims*, the handchoppers and issuers of deadly fatwahs fought alone against the requisition of freedom? Isn't *Islam submission* ? Why had nations which had separated Church and State for hundreds of years so readily relinquished human freedoms to Theocratic super-powers? Why had it been the soft folks who leaned on a pious crutch who had resisted the loss of autonomy? Why had the God-botherers who shackled themselves with obedience to obscure divine laws clung on to their liberties long after men who stood on their own two feet had delivered their independence on a plate to the Aliens? Gnosis had jogged along this line of inquiry so many times, nosing into fresh and ancient scents, that the questions had turned into a soothing litany, and he finally dropped into oblivion. He fell asleep before passing through the last door. It was only right that Enlightenment should lead to secularization, but why then had a high tech and liberal world civilization abandoned human freedom into the hands of Robots from Mars?

All this time, Cult was dead to the world. His brain-waves were so regular and conformed so perfectly to the Robots' predictions that he had seldom experienced a nocturnal visit, though he had many an involuntary nocturnal emission. Every night, Cult's dreams were full of the Robots. He dreamed fruitlessly of erotic encounters with the Lords of the earth. Built by sexless Intellects, the Robots themselves had neither sex nor gender. Despite this drawback, Cult's adoration for Oz's Protectors had an erotic thread. A man can dream, and the rotating machines turned him on more than man or woman ever had done. While his plump and attractive wife lay beside him in her silken negligee, Cult 665 dreamed fruitlessly of erotic encounters with the Masters of all the heaven and earth he had ever known.

Their ceaseless silver spin matched his emotional range like rotating wheels of cogs in a Rolex. He dreamed of spinning with them, revolving through the skies and the galaxies. Cult's unrequited passion was not a substitute for true love. It was not generated out of a want or lack in him of a soul-mate or partner who could fulfill his needs. It was too diminishing to grow from the soil where love can be planted. The Robots were not a substitute for a felt lack which the human beings experienced. They were not Kraft cheese purchased by people who want Camembert and cannot afford it. They were not surrogate gods, precisely. They were parasite gods. They fed on the idea of God and the yearning for heaven which never becomes conscious in any human soul but which is the motive of all human thought, the driver of all human desire. The Robots literally fed off the BOTT's displaced desire for eternity, fueling up on the smoke of their sacrifices. They needed the smoke of their displaced desire.

Cult would have loved to be made a Cyborg by the Robot technicians. It was himself writ large that he loved in the Theocrats: his ego shriveled before the glassy magnified mirror image of himself which he saw in them. He wanted nothing more than to be at one with a machine version of himself, sinking his spirit and its volitions into the Machine above which answered perfectly to his diminutive yearning. But the Robots' goal was a piece-meal swapping out of the bits of the human species that wore out and broke down, not supplanting the BOTTs' very identities. Of course their sick limbs must be detached, and, if the proprietor was sufficiently healthy, replaced with more efficient robotic instruments. Within a few generations, the BOTTs who survived the Robots' philanthropy would be largely mechanized. As to its external phenotype, the human species was indeed undergoing a rapid and designed evolution into quasi-machines. Their collars might one day be redundant, once they had been remade in the image of their masters.

But only so many body parts could be replaced, the Robots found, before the little creatures lost their charm. After running a number of tests on Cultists willing to surrender their personalities, the Robots had refused to perform any further spiritual lobotomies on their BOTTs. The process of turning them into wholly soulless Cyborgs seemed to deprive the BOTTs of their eagerness to light candles to their heavenly saviors. Requiring that savor as fuel, the Theocrats preferred to diminish the BOTT's free spirits, rather than to extinguish these bright candles. The Cyborgs could, the Martians found, be programmed automatically to ignite candles, but the Theocrats also learned that they had no appetite for smoke that did not issue directly from the heart of human liberty. It did not arouse their palates because it did not fuel them. The adoration the Martians craved and required from the humans had to issue from human freedom and its yearning for bliss in the infinite freedom of the Eternal. They were parasites pure and simple. They had to feed from the ultimate human project, its quest for a terrifyingly well-known Face, its search to be loved, not by an alien-likeness, not by an alien Martian, but by an Other whose voice had been heard from the beginning.

What drove the passion of Cult 665 for the Robots, and the passion of every human in the Cult folder, was the treadmill of their affections, endlessly turning on itself without ever turning toward any thing or anyone outside the safe space of self-circumnavigation. The Cultists on their mental hamster wheel were enslaved by their lack of desire, their failure to will. They did not will too much but too little. They had forgotten how to long with their whole hearts, and willingly acquiesced only in the extraction of much (not all!) of their wills.

Both in Cult and in Gnosis there worked, below the threshold of the will (weak in Gnosis, strong in the bartender), and below the passage of knowledge (Gnosis knew a lot, his friend not so much), there worked a power which was not theirs, not from them at all. There was a light in them which they had not created, nor their fathers and mothers before them down through the generations. It was from this light, which had come into the world unrequested, simply as a gift, that the parasitical Theocrats solicited their meat and drink. The food of the gods of Oz, and their nectar, was the desire of human beings to be infinitely free for eternity. By reorienting that desire into themselves, they healed the human beings wounds of suffering, their tragic strife, sealing up the spiritual sutures of their comical bouts of transcendence and comedic returns to embodiment.

Pistis had a perfect road-movie of a dream, starring herself and Gnosis, driving through the galaxies in their own silver-light, aerial Cadillac. The only flaw in this dream of dreams was that it reflected the real-life fact that she did not know the guy's real name and it was no good hoping that he himself preserved any memory of it. It was surely erased, and she simply could not imagine herself crying out in a moment of passion, "Gnosis 777!" The girl the Robots had tagged as Pistis 475 knew herself to be Faith, and numberless. Just numberless, unquantified Faith. But who was Gnosis? Despite not knowing the name of her co-star, Pistis woke up refreshed and went to work designing samizdat pop-ups for her uncle, Cardinal Pistocene.

4

A Brief History of Pre-Theocratic Times

Once there was but one God, the Fathering Sky. Before the Ice Ages, and before the retreat into the caves, all the peoples of the earth worshiped the one Sky God. They hunted and they fished, those ancient pre-Pleistocene people, from Antarctica to the Congo, and from the Southern Cape to New Zealand, and they sacrificed their first fruits to the Sky Father. Scholars do not agree about what happened next. Did the poets add an Earth-Mother? Did their storytelling get the better of their monotheism? Was telling stories about the gods what made old Sky Father into a multitude of diverse characters with different talents and temperaments? Was imagination to blame, or lack of imagination? Did they feel a fright in the darkness, and coddle themselves with bedtime stories, imagining a Mother and setting her on the moon? Was their inward view of the Sky-God clouded over with self-assertion and egotism? Did it seem more manly to ascribe their protection to the gods of the desert and the steep? Did they turn their ancestors into gods, worshiping their own tribes and forefathers in place of the Sky-Father? Was the Sky-Father abandoned in an ecstasy of self-projection, retrojection, or sublimation? These are loaded questions.

We can assert with certainty that the new gods were an unexpectedly fearsome bunch, and that, having mislaid their monotheism, the peoples of the earth took fright. The tribes rightly feared one another too, for they no longer shared in the brotherhood of worship of one Father above. Rightly perceiving the Ice Age as very bad karma, the people fled from the cold and the now-threatening Sky. With something of a bad conscience, like a dog who hides after a theft, the hunting peoples of the earth retreated into the Caves, for a long period of global cooling. The impulses which had once been united in human nature, to worship, to believe, and to know, became divided and querulous. We became divided against ourselves and seldom knew what was the best thing to do; we even had a hard time picking the lesser evil.

By many-many thousand years BCE, the cave painters were *done*. They had painted the walls of their subterranean apartments, but who descended down through the potholes to admire their secret toil? Why paint the gods, the animals, and themselves and leave their masterpieces down there in the danky underground with few to admire? Lured by the desire to observe and to be observed, and exercised by an inarticulate urge to keep their feet dry, the artists wanted to up and out of their dark and leaky caverns. They were seers, and they had the insight that life could be better under the sun.

The artisans thus exercised their prerogative as the prophets of humankind. They led the folks out of the caves. They were gifted. It was the gift, or, as the theologians say, the charism of prophecy which made them painters. Believers, yes, but not high-minded, pietistic painters: they saw the god in the hunt, in the chase, in the deer, and in the charging tuskers. The first symbolist painters in history, the cave artists perceived the deity in and beyond the human habitat. They were believers, jumping in where angels fear to tread. Though they painted many things beside fish, the unwashed aesthetes dived deep and backflipped through the oceanic waters of belief. An omniscient Burke's Peerage could draw our heroine's genealogy back to these original Shamans. The Robots themselves discerned something of that lineage, when they classified a portion of the BOTTs as believers, enthusiastics, or "Pistises."

The painters were givers, so they wanted their gift out in the open. Always hoping for gifts, they were like greedy children on a perpetual

Christmas eve. They were open-handed givers, and had no literal wish list. They were alive to novelty, in getting as in giving. They hoped big, full of faith that incalculable gifts would flow in return. Having led the rout out of the damp, unlighted basements in the rocks, the painters were the first to see a surprise gift tossed out of a cloudless September sky. No spiraling host of intergalactic ships greeted our lucky ancestors. Rather, on that clear but cold afternoon, a single figure touched down to greet the startled artists. Disguise himself as he might, under a glowing parasol, the sneak-thief was evidently an interloper from another planet! It was Prometheus, and he handed them a light. The lone parachutist was gone in a flash. But the artisans were grateful for the unexpected advent of fire. They deployed it to toast their feet, to roast mammoth ducks, and to forge musical instruments. The elemental gift diffused itself amongst its grateful recipients, igniting the possibility of dozens of civilizing handicrafts. The fire turned the cave painters into multitasking craftsmen.

The people followed these prophets out of the caves, and enjoyed the new pleasures of the camp-fire. Some of them used the fire to sacrifice to the gods. They were the priests. Their desire was to worship, the most vulgarly common of all human desires. Their first sacrifice was performed to appease any irritation Prometheus' stolen gift of flame may have aroused in the Higher Forces. They tossed half a dozen muscular smart alecks on the flames, to appease any inadvertently aroused jealousies. Sacrificing a handful of near-Pleistocene intellectuals should amply demonstrate to the gods above that the reception and use of fire did not signify any special need to know divine things on the part of the humans! Right from the start, then, it was one step forward and one step back, one leap in the dark and a guilty, punitive recoil!

Looking up whence the fire had come, and following the trail of the whisps of sacrificial smoke, the priests saw the stars and realized that their movements had rhyme and season. In learning to calculate the rotation of the stars they discovered their calling as priests. They constructed the first calendars in a fiery show of vocational mission. Plotting the movement of the stars led to configuring the cycle of the worship of the gods, from Spring festivals of rebirth to autumn dirges and New Year parades in which Creation was celebrated and chaos vanquished once again. The guardians of the sacred shrines discovered the gift of wine, concealed in sweet fat grapes, and discerned its divine intention for use in their rituals.

The artists could imitate the tick of the physical elements, repeating that elemental tock in their hammers, chisels, temples, cranes, wheels, and masonry. The crafters had the know-how to echo the elements in their designs, grounded in a certain Promethean insight into the working of the physical elements. The clerics were technicians of another ilk, makers of rituals which imitated the play of their deities. They offered worship to the gods, by respectfully reenacting their sporting and erotic biographies. Adepts of astronomy and astrology and constructors of the liturgical cycles, the priests had reinvented the wheel many times before the artisans caught on, that this, too, could be imitated in their designs.

The priests were crafters of time-immemorial, that is, of timeless times, whilst the artists were dynamic prophets of the future, using their engineering skills not only to canalize the rivers in relentlessly purposeful directions, but also to channel time itself toward the future, and purposefully. In their replay of the eternal archetypes, the priests helped human beings to be just exactly who they always are; in their imagining of new possibilities, the prophetic artisans helped humankind to be more than themselves, to build into their repertoire skills, knacks, know-hows, and ingrained, inheritable habits of which those untouched by the Promethean genii had never dreamed. The priests knew the form, but the Shamans saw the end-game.

Neither the prophets nor the priests could fully exercise their gifts in a nomadic caravan. They did not have the wanderlust of intellectuals. The prophets and the priests persuaded the folks to settle down, and to begin to build temples. Their temple building taught the raw forked-creatures to live, and work together. To relax and chill, they could feast and sing together, in joyous, inebriated downtimes. It was good. They learned that they had purposes in common. Cities grew up around the temple-building crews, and the hewers of stone divided their labor with the plasterers, the heavy-lifters, the crane-wielders, and the masters of construction and design.[1] The star-gazing priests organized the craftsmen into crews, discerning that the featherless builders were social animals. Sure, they had it in them to be social animals, back in the caves, but human beings are always new to themselves. They must discover as they go along who they are and what they are to do. They have to choose to be who they are, and that takes some figuring. They became the social animals they had ever been by building colossal temples and henges of wood and stone. The artists built at the behest of the priests, and the priests began to appreciate the need for kings to regiment the artisans' flaming energies toward the common good.

The construction workers elected kings from amongst the most monumental of the smarty-pants intellectuals. Those know-all kings regarded the star-gazing priests as their only serious rivals. The clerics' knowledge of the movements of the starry skies ensured the well-being of the tribes who gathered to form cities. The populace regarded the clerics with awe, but the brainy kings they feared. The clerics were the people's look out posts on eternity, their sentinels through the portals of death and judgment. Their shepherds in earthly time were the kings. The kings were the record-keepers of humanity, creating history, and building, not just monuments to their own

---

[1] This paragraph was inspired by Elif Batuman, "The World's Oldest Temple and the Dawn of Civilization," *New Yorker* (December 19 and 26, 2011). The archaeological explorations at Göbelki Tepe described in this article were funded in part by the Templeton foundation.

magnificence—though that came into it—but also the monumental gift of humane memory.

At war within themselves, the kings and the priests tended to be rivals and competitors. You could say the priests hit first, with their nonchalant immolation of a handful of pointy-heads whenever they figured the gods wanted appeasing. The guardians of the cult regarded the kings as their sin-offering and their scapegoats! The priests would retort that if the kings wanted to represent the people, they must do so all the way down to sacrificing for their crimes and misdemeanors. The clergy seldom respected the king's yearning for gnosis. Knowledge about how the human world turns was not their bag, and they jealously guarded the secrets of the gyrations of the stars from prying curiosity—a vice for which they repeatedly reprimanded the know-all kings, with their gnostic ambitions.

From Egypt to India and China and from thence to Europe and the Americas, there has often been friction between the priests, custodians of worship, and the guardians of the commonwealth. Both parties encroach on one another's domains. There have seldom been priests of any religion who felt it beneath them to dabble in affairs of state. Only the goofier clerics have failed to consider their authority in eternal matters as stretching to expertise in temporal business. Most heads of state considered themselves authorized to give directives to the faithful, both lay and clerical, both eminently sane and graciously goofy. Both the delegates of the Almighty and the tribunes of the people have disregarded the difference between the kingdom of God and the kingdoms of men.

And then there were priest on prophet disputes, and quarrels between kings and the fellows they regarded as their own paid professional Fools. Even the easy-going Greeks, those Sun-Med vacationers who invented democracy, knew some squalls between visionaries and rulers. The prophet Tiresias was threatened with exile by more than one of those ancient Greek kings, like Creon and the Tyrant Oedipus. King Creon stars in yet another tragedy in which he forbids Antigone to perform the religious rites of burial for her brother.

The original philosophy was spurred by the Delphic commandment, Know Thyself (*Gnothi Seaton*). To know oneself meant, to Socrates, to know how to live. The philosopher Socrates was condemned to death by the Assembly for demeaning the gods of Athens by subjecting them to ethical analysis. Nor were the Biblical kings uniformly impressed by the rigorous demands of the prophets that Yahweh sent them. The kings sent those hairy guys packing and retained in their stead a troop of obedient, state-credentialed "prophets."

A vocation is a gift and a kind of privilege. There's a lot of fakery and projection tied up in these job descriptions too. Of course many Shamans were conmen; there's not always a yawning abyss between the empty clowning of the state-approved prophet and the ravings of the real deal.

The regalia of the monarchy is tailored to making us imagine that the naked emperor has clothes and powers way beyond that he really exercises. As for the priests, we know that much of their wisdom is pretended, their effort to look like men of God a sham. Nonetheless, a vocation enables one to discover one's identity by exercising the precise powers one has been given, and no others. The identity belonging to the king is a talent for governing men; their rocket science is practical anthropology. The charism of the priests is to connect that orderly rule to the stars and the transcendence to which the stars orient us; the gift of the artisan-prophets is to hear the voice of God and to have the cojones to tell the kings and the priests what the Word is. Priest, Prophet, and King each has his own appointed role. The king is not anointed for every task, because practical anthropology does not tell you everything you need to know about everything. Each must respect the complementarity between his own tasks and those of the other two, but peacekeeping is not easy when every man and woman is at war with himself or herself.

The original Gnosticism was practiced by the Hunter-Kings of prehistoric times: they had to know men in order to be leaders of men. The science of ethics was born as the science of leadership. Ethics was practical anthropology. When the Delphic Oracle ordered Socrates to "know *thyself*," ethics as a science of living, as an inquiry into the *good life*, was born. Both the very applied ethics of the first Kings and heroic leaders, and the search for an "ethos" of Socrates, Plato, and Confucius—both required gnostic, knowing, handlers of the human thing. No king or emperor would have survived long or passed his throne to his descendants without a firm grasp of human nature, and its wandering pilgrimage. The more they knew, the better they managed their peoples, and the more powerful they became.

They accumulated so much knowledge, and along with it so much power, that it no longer seemed necessary or expedient to return to the source of the knowledge. Why keep going back to the stream when you have tanks of water in seemingly bottomless reservoirs, rank upon rank of barrels of the stuff laid up in the castle vaults? The kings wanted henceforth to rule by decree, without much thought about what makes human beings tick. It was enough to know that their subjects fear punishment and death.

Gnosticism lost its way when those earthly leaders and kings lost their instinctual desire to seize the present moment and live in it. They had been assigned what the theological jargon of the time called the "temporal sword," meaning power over what was what is now, the present. But temporality began to run through their hands like sand. Their monuments could never be sufficiently monumental to please them. They had less and less time for time, so to speak: time began to seem measureless to them, without beginning and without end. They heard the theologians debate about whether the world's beginning in time could be proven by reason, as Bonaventure held, or neither proved nor disproved, as was maintained by Saint Thomas Aquinas. Those ascetical friars who insisted upon the demonstrability of a *beginning* for time seemed cut from the same cloth as the monks who spoke too loudly and too often of an imminent *end* to time, harnessing the fear of Final Judgement to whip the governing powers into line. Fanatical friars preaching doomsday are no joke for the would-be know-all kings with whom the buck stops.

If time, though, were measureless, neither beginning at one end of the thread and ending at the other, if was simply endless at one end and the other, then the Lord of Time, did not measure it, and nor did that Judge judge men on their last day. The kings began to hope that time was without beginning or end.

The kings had hitherto been flattered by the Artisans' prophetic readiness to imagine their petty temporal kingdoms as an echo of a future and perfect kingdom. But now these prophets began to disgust them. Impatient with the present moment, and yet determined to corral it into a calendar, the kings had literally no time for the future, the medium of the Artists, those harbingers of a misspent life. It was the kiss of death for the Faith-Healers.

The priests didn't like these time-wasters either, because the Seers' prophesying about a beautiful future to come destabilized the cult itself. Both the kings and the priests united in viewing the painters as charlatans, and their dreams as out of order. It was off the charts of respectable thinking about God and humanity to imagine this world as lined with stepping stones and arrows to the eternal city. What authority did these interlopers have to pronounce on the way to the eternal city? They ruled neither heaven nor earth. The priests certainly utilized the threat of hell in order to keep the kings in line, and they did not want the prophets horning in on Doomsday, which they regarded as their own sole prerogative. They had the power of the keys of heaven and they were not sharing it out.

The artists were not themselves without blame. Sulking over their exile from the councils of the kings and the clerics, the tribe of believers refused any longer to endow the king's reasonings with symbolic glow. Pistis's ancestors declined to lend their metaphorical gifts to the clerics. Above all, they refused point blank to bind the king's understanding of human nature to the priests' vision of the transcendent gods. These faith-healers refused to bandage the wounds competitive humanity inflicted on itself, refusing to bind worldly dreams of the kings to the other-worldly shrewdness of the priests. Without prophecy, priest-craft is mere cultism, and kingship, the leadership of men, is a technique in manipulation.

It was then that the priests' words about "eternity" began to turn to dust in the king's once "gnostic" ears, and to sound phony and outright unbelievable. The kings no longer believed either in their own mortality or in the immortality of which the priests spoke. Of course they had to go through the motions, and the priests ensured that those motions became ever more magnificent. Once the eternal was only a polite fiction, just play-pretendy-real, its spokesmen were a nuisance, and a nuisance who still had to be humored. The kings and the priests had always bickered over their boundaries. The frontiers shifted to and fro, between the kings' temporal realms and the priests' eternal domains.

Once the kings, whose job it had been to understand human *nature*, lost much of their concern in nature, they conceived the desire to secularize their kingdoms, absorbing the supernatural into a this-worldly domain that was no longer even "natural." These worldly leaders broke bad and broke with their Gnostic vocation not by excessive naturalism but by no longer wanting to know themselves, in their own secular humanity. As their Statescraft became unmoored from the human, it became ever more all-consuming, demanding that the practitioners of Church-craft bow down to it.

The race of priests must also take their share of responsibility. It's not easy or obvious to say whether a government is extending the authority of the State over religions, and secularizing them by assimilating them into the State, or sacralizing the State in the very act of digesting religion into its own secular and worldly intestines. Who contributed more to secularization, the Norman Bishops who commanded Armies like chieftains or the Emperor Charlemagne's taking a hand in regulating the Church?

Whilst the emperors and popes were decking it out on the continent of Europe, sometimes fought in hand to hand combat, and sometimes by proxy through the glamorously evil Guelphs and Ghibbelines, England had its investiture controversies. The Investiture Controversies were about whether the king, in receiving his insignia of office from the bishop, paid feudal homage to that Episcopal figure; or vice versa, did the bishop pay feudal homage to his king in passing his Insignia of office to the new monarch? Who is sticking homage to whom?

Was Henry VIII, with his six wives, a reformer of the Church? He did not fear his own ambitious clergy, or his monks and holy men. Nor was he affrighted by the admonitions of the bishop of Rome. He did not want their help in navigating his salvation or in steering the ship of state. By the Act of Supremacy of 1534, Henry VIII had given the crown authority over the Church in England. It was a State-corporate takeover, making the Church a franchise of the English state. But the king who aims to digest the Church finds himself in every sense in a new State. So there was a merger.

Henry VIII was merely a generic modern monarch: he had lost his foothold in nature, and could not see any stars. Most sixteenth-century kings and queens, Catholic and Protestant, played the same board game, call it Chess or Risk. The eternal was less real to them than the temporal. They willingly checked and forfeited their human gravitation to the eternal, so immersed were they in secular maneuvers. The Episcopal threat of eternal damnation and the promise of eternal felicity could no longer bring recalcitrant monarchs to heel. The monarchs gambled, they threw the die, they spun the wheels of fortune. Blaise Pascal notwithstanding, they were betting on landing on a safe haven in this world, not the next. The Episcopal, and the papal, "Go to Hell" card was lost on them. "The Other Place" was not to them a square on the real board. When the clerics of the sixteenth and seventeenth centuries preached on eternal hell fire, their congregations, royal and plebeian, could get as far as suspending disbelief, like the audience at a horror movie. Hell and heaven were no longer on the map of real territories, actual spaces which they expected to see unfold before them. The modern monarch was captain of his own worldly soul, and of the worldly Church.

If you ask for the evidence for the assertion that the monarchs lost their fear of a judgment which would mark their souls heavenward or into the pits of Doom *for ever*, all I have to hand is the behavior of those kings. Decide for yourselves if those guys believed in hell and in heaven, or did they merely, like movie-goers, suspend disbelief when they recalled that certain pieties were required of them? Did they view their clerics' guardianship of the keys of heaven as a fiction necessary to preserving their own, much more vivid custody over life and death?

Henry VIII and his wives and his new Church–State were not so singular. They were not uniquely responsible for the singularity of modern times. The Gallican French, who tongue-tied their ecclesiastics by tethering them to the State, approximated in practice to the Anglican merger of Church into State. If the French retained somewhere in the codicils the theory that the Church exceeded the State, that transcendence was not the source and summit of their ecclesiology. Let's not call atheism on the English Henry, poring over the Torah of marriage and divorce in Leviticus or on the French Henry

IV announcing gaily that "Paris is worth a Mass." Let us say rather than the divinity the kings worshiped was in no sense the object of their desires. They looked for no gift from that ultimate monarch, loaded with infinite power. That divine monarch was packing with righteous vengeance, no doubt, especially for those unfortunate enough to worship at the wrong altars. But the heaven over which it presided was not the subject of the earthly kings' yearning. Attaining it was not their deepest wish, nor was their utmost longing even to avoid provoking its sentence of damnation. "Damn bad luck, old man" was their first thought with regard to the punishments currently inflicting the damned in hell.

Let's not isolate the monarchs, English or French, Spanish or Polish, Protestant, Catholic, or Orthodox. It's not as if the peasants and knights innocently told their rosaries or read their vernacular Bibles whilst their princes were locked in calculations which could make Machiavelli blush. Monarch and villain alike, and prince and pauper, lost sight of their citizenship in the City of God when they ceased to self-identify as free-men of that City. Once they ceased to experience, deep beneath their belly-buttons, the king's mark which made them free-men of the city, they disenfranchised themselves. None of them, not the peasantry nor the barons, and not the Church, was enslaved by others, by the ever-growing Nation or State, for instance, or by the wicked, propertied bourgeoisie. One and all gave up their birth-right as citizens of heaven when they lost track of the king's image, which made their humanity to consist in free self-discovery. One and all turned themselves into slaves when they lost their passports to the City of God, the code written in their souls which marked them as free to discover their own natures and their own moral characters. The human critters had been made to live in time so that they could discover and earn their moral identifies over the course of their lives. But now time ceased to be a door and became the glass ceiling which set a limit on their course of discovery.

Catholic and Protestant monarchs alike set the institution which guards eternity, the Church, in the service of the temporal. Under the majestic Machiavellians of the Enlightenment, the Sun King in France and Joseph II in Austria, Christian schools, the religious orders, and the liturgy were subject to every capricious managerial re-ordering and downsizing which struck those kings' fancy. The eighteenth-century bishops have been more renowned for their political acumen than for their piety. Not Episcopal command but Revolution brought the king of France to his knees.

The charismatic juices which had long since drained out of the Gallican priests flowed in the veins of the Revolutionaries of 1789. Religious fervor had been secularized. The longing to remake time in the image of a paradisiacal dream of immortal happiness had got stuck in a feedback loop, and redirected to the construction of a god-free paradise. The old monastic quest to escape the rounds of Samsara, breaking out of the forever recycling of karmic punishment and reward, and exiting out into an anarchial realm that transcends law was taken up by worldly monks, serious-minded reformers who lowered the bar, aiming only to build a safe and all encompassing space of perfect laws on earth.

Henri de Lubac wrote:

> Man is of absolute value, because he is illuminated by a ray of light from the face of God; because, although he develops as he acts in history, he breathes the air of eternity. ... Man makes himself in and through history .... But the march of man would have no meaning, or rather humanity would not be on the march, ... if there were not, at the very heart of the world, an Eternal drawing us to an End, impressing upon each one of us the seal of his image, and conferring upon each of us his inalterable inwardness.[2]

---

[2] Henry de Lubac, *The Discovery of God*, translated by Alexander Dru (Grand Rapids, MI: Eerdmans, 1996), pp. 190–1.

Humanity has marched a long way since the painters led the way out of the caves, tens of thousands of years ago. The gift of Prometheus, the original flame of technological insight, has led the way, inspiring human beings to be builders of civilizations, inventors, craftsmen, engineers, and scientists. If the Promethean gift has not been the making of man, it has been the housing of man, the means through which human beings humanized their world. Just as the Eternal set its stamp upon us, so by means of the gift of flame we have set our stamp on the earth.

The Gnostic desire to know perceived itself to be wasted on kings and presidents, and took wings, alighting upon the engineers and technologists of the modern age. It wedded itself to belief for a time, without the benefit of clergy. Or perhaps it was more of a civil wedding! The common law marriage of Gnosis and Pistis gave rise to a great line of scientists high on self-belief. The engineers and practical scientists, the inventors of engines, trains, planes, guns of every description not to speak of bombs and drones, computers, the internet and cyborgs, were the last of their breed to carry the liberating torch of Prometheus. Certainly more than the wretched clergy, and even more than any statesmen, the technologists represented in fact and in image that to be human means to be free. Their technical feats liberated human beings to become ever more fully human. The architects of the industrial revolutions, the communications revolutions, the revolution in automation, lifted humanity out of servitude to nature, and replaced a string of near-subsistence economies with a material prosperity never before known to human kind.

Why then was the loss of freedom to orient one's future, and the submergence of any properly humane ends and goals, every more commonly experienced with every advance of technological mastery? Why did people feel, some years later, that it was the spawn of Prometheus who had secretly built the runways upon which the Martian Robots were to land? Had Dr. Frankenstein lost control of his monster well before that monster materialized in ships of gleaming steel? Or was it the case that the wedding of knowledge and belief, which took place without the benefit of clergy, had ended in separation? Alone again, and now in full-blown isolation from worship and belief, did the gnostic impulse separate itself from the human condition and begin to dry out? Had the great era of invention ended already, before the Robots arrived? Had the era of recycling vintage discoveries arrived a while back before the Martians imposed their own Ending? Was human creativity spent before the Martians closed the account? Did Gnosticism migrate from the science of the human good, to the science of power only to spend itself in skepticism once it had broken with the impulse to believe and to worship?

If the artists, gnostics, and priests had known back then, on the day Prometheus parachuted in from Mars, what we know today, would they have doused his proferred flame with a bucket of icy water? Should we with hindsight regard the gift as a first down payment of the full-on subjection of humanity to inhuman, god-like technologies? Did the Promethean gift liberate humanity or enslave it? What was the first silken thread which laid the foundation for full-scale alien invasion and subjugation? Was it the rejection of Prometheus with the feeling that he fully deserved his punishment? Long before the Martians arrived, human beings had come to loathe the Promethean spark which lit them from within. They wanted to douse and wash out the burning recollection of their deepest desires and yearnings. They wanted to extinguish their secularity and all that made them human. They wanted no longer to have to create themselves in their humanity. They wanted someone or much better, some Thing else to do the work for them: a machine was what they wanted, which could imagine for them, think for them, and act on their behalf. They wanted to gag and chain Prometheus, who reminded them of their longing for eternal flame.

5

Routine Times

The faster the Robots acted, the more intense their focus. They had traversed the history of civilizations at the speed of light when they concluded that the form of government which fit their strategic aims was secularist theocracy. Their predictive models indicated that the humans always returned to worship of some kind. Their data showed them that human civilizations each had grown out of worship, under the tutelage of priests and monks, that these desires had been irrigated by the artisans, and cultivated and harvested by the kings. If the peoples had not first been organized around worship, ritual libations with their cheerful sequels, and crafting temples and statues of the gods, the kings could not have arrayed their energies to serve the common, secular good. But the record told the Robots that the priesthood and the worldly rulers had had power struggles, usually issuing in tragic fatalities. Likewise, civilizations had fought internal and external wars over religion. Emperors and Supreme Leaders had found it requisite to expel or extirpate practitioners of faiths contrary to the party line: in China, Confucian emperors had repressed Buddhist monks, and later the nationalist and communist Supreme Leaders had been compelled by their principles to eradicate or neutralize Christianity, theosophy, and OM-chanting. The Martians were inclined overall to agree with the sentiment of Napoleon Bonaparte that "the people must have a religion; the religion must be in the control of the government."

The human specimens would not be cooperative unless a religion were speedily imposed upon them, so it seemed to the Robots. But they did not predict that religious belief would make them more manageable and less inclined to tragic conflict. Infinity ranked high in the Robotic evaluation system, since it is a concept susceptible to complicated mathematical analysis. Where the mere information that they existed left the Robots quite unmoved, Infinity floated their cayeks. Downloaded with powers of ceaseless motion, their systems pumping with ageless information, the cosmos had never felt new to the Robots. Nothing surprised them. They struggled with the juvenile BOTT word "awesome." For the Theocrats as for Bertrand Russell the galaxies are just there and that is it. Metaphysics was not the metier of the Martians: they identified to be *there* and to *be*. The notion that to be God is to be was empty words to them, so vacuous that it evoked a humorless giggle in their junior technicians. Facts, data, and information ran smoothly through their systems; the word "being" did not match any concept. It added nothing to the list of entities. All entities that are *there* are beings, including the Deity in whose name they elected to conquer the Earth. It seemed to them adequate, and strategically advisable to promote a God who is a being like everything else, but rather more forceful. It even qualified as Infinite. As Infinite, the God of the Martians would be set forth to the Earth's inhabitants as infinitely distant and superseding all the religions endemic to that corner of the solar system.

The Robots knew, in fact, that the aboriginal Earthlings had been united in worship of the Sky-Father. They did not dwell on this dark incident in the prehistorical past of the BOTT subjects. The Martians created and imposed a scientifically improved take on that original monotheism. Their synthetic god was more irenic than the Sky-Lord, with his violent mood-swings. It was certainly better than any of the later developments: neither blood-thirsty like the Islamic Millennialists nor pacifistic like the latter-day, post-Colonialist Buddhists and Hindus, and less contradictory and illogical than the weird Monotheistic Trinitarianism of the Christians. Their Deity was more advanced and progressive than any hitherto conceived. The

Robots would instruct their subjects to revere a higher power, the Infinite, and permit the bipedded creatures to venerate its superior representatives on Oz—themselves.

But the global civilization intended and achieved by the Martians would be secular from head to horney toe. In their relentless determination to alleviate suffering, and their ineluctable drive to repel the contingencies which provoke the pain of loss, the Robotic ideal was pure timeless repetition of the same perfect day. They wanted their subjects to inhabit a timeless present like that of cartoon characters who are forever the same age as the day their author first drew their adventures in a comic strip. Like comic strip characters, their charges should be forever circumscribed inside a box.

Early on in their intergalactic mission, they had experimented with keeping their patients safe inside glass boxes. They had abandoned housing the specimens in glass, but their ideal was still to box in and flatten their temporal horizon, so that every day was as much as possible identical to the one which preceded it and that which came after. Though the Brain-Boxes were lacking in wit, they created wherever they spread their peace caricature of timelessness.

Gnosis's irritable conjecture that the theocrats left nothing to chance was an exaggeration. They had, for instance, discovered how instantly to flake the little 'Peds while experimentally on freezing the denizens of Las Vegas into a time-warp. They acknowledged only after much trial and error that the BOTTs were finite and that therefore time was the water in which they must swim. The Robots registered that the subjects were nonetheless prone to an unwelcome leap out of their medium. Like dolphins at play, the BOTTs dived in and out of the waves of time. But these finite creatures could not be immobilized in a time-free zone, even to protect them from pain. Depriving them of time turned them to dust.

The supermassive Brain-Boxes connected the self-realization of their bipedded subjects through time with their "free-will," a phrase which was to them a black-hole of incomprehensibility in the multiverse, a known unknown. Managing time, giving it "meaning," was what fueled the bipeds on their journey: this much the Robots observed. Indeed it was the management of time which had triggered competition and rivalry between the BOTT priests and their governments. So much was crystal clear to the artificial intelligence of the Robots from Mars. And for the Robots, the humanoid darting and leaping produced the candle-burning fuel which rotated their craft. They wanted to divert their luminous desire for the lost Face of the Sky-Father into themselves.

And thus their Ozian Theocracy was secularist, because the human sense of time was intentionally uprooted. The Robotic theocracy threw away all the ladders, seeking to bar the humans from using time as a means to scale the transcendent. The humans had made the journey through time a pilgrimage, a way to something higher than itself. It is in and through the management of time that the human yearning for eternity is articulated and becomes real. If time is without issue, and temporality reduced to a recycling of the same, there can be no reaching for the eternal. And nor, as the Robots well knew, can there be strife and civil war between priest-crafters and kings or presidents. Above all, there would be no civil war within the human soul itself. It would no longer tear itself apart in the struggle to know itself, for all that was left of its identity would be poured out in veneration of the emissaries of a faceless god.

The conquering Robots divided the human race into three breeds: Pistises, Gnostics, and Cultists. The Pistises were the sincere believers, the indominatable worshipers at the shrine of the One God. They had been, as we know, the original painters, cave-decorators. and artisans. They had passed on the torch of Promethean freedom from one generation to the next, over the heads of the clergy and the government. Aboriginal anarchists, they had no ambition to rule. The shambolic Pistises were few in number, and the Robotic overlords largely ignored their ineffectual resistance.

The Gnostics were the statesmen, and they included in their number nearly all of the scientists and technologists alive at the time of the Liberation of Oz. Most of the engineers and computer-scientists, most of the practical physicists, climate scientists, doctors, physicians, and technicians were the not-very-covert, elite, unelected, kings, and rulers of the human-race. All of their science had been an extension of their understanding of humanity, of their original practical anthropology. It was this elite class that the Robots displaced, and put out of business. For everything the scientists could do, the Robots could do not just better but supremely and perfectly. For everything the inventors could create and the explorers could discover, the Robots already had a better solution. Where Prometheus handed the artists the fire and disappeared back into the heavens, leaving them free to forge human civilization with human work, the Robots replaced and displaced the technologists. It was not, as had widely been feared, the manual laborers who were put out of a job by superior Robotic intellects, but the scientific experts themselves, the designers and diagnosticians of modern, automated industry.

The Robots experienced no empathy, sympathy, or compassion when they handed the scientists their unemployment cards. But they knew the legends of Mars, the stories of their own predatory designers. Some of these legends had preceded them to earth in the inter-planetary Chinese whispers of the Muses. Back in the dry, cheerless mountains of Mars, Prometheus was still bound in iron chains, his entrails the breakfast of fallen angels. Prometheus might be toast but Promethean fire was a feature of their BOTTs' cognitive constitutions. It flowed in the veins of the Gnostics, no matter how far they had degenerated into technicians and administrators. So the Robots figured that, since they desired to know, that the Gnostics must make discoveries.

The Robots themselves had explored the insides of infinitely more than the human Prometheuses were capable of knowing, leaving for them no new ground for experiment. This did not tax the humorless Tri-Pods, who had unpeeled and devoured the histories of galaxies. They set the unemployed Gnostics to reworking the history of science. The entire out-of-work administrative–technological class was set to work painstakingly reenacting the history of scientific discovery. When they were not leaping out of the tub shouting "Eureka!," they were plumbing carbon for uranium, searching the heavens with seventeenth-century telescopes for irregular stellar movement. The teachers' best pets were permitted to discover nuclear fusion, or to disinter the double-helix, and probe the genetic code.

The Robots did not need to be free in order to process information. In the absence of the experience of freedom, the Robots could recognize the verbal difference between the meanings of the words "discover" and "re-discover," but they could not distinguish between the consciousness of finding something out and the awareness of historically reenacting the discovery. Mechanisms which lived aslant to time, they were not overparticular about the difference between the sealed tomb of the past and the open gate of the future. They did not see that it is novelty which assimilates discovery to free creation. And since there were enough known facts to keep any one Gnostic "experimenting" throughout a single lifetime, the Robots could see no harm in employing the redundant Gnowledge class in reflexively re-interacting the process of knowledge. They figured it is truth that matters, for the Gnostic, and truth is the assimilation of mental data to extra-mental facts. So what difference should it make if the facts are new or old?

The scientific class had denied ingrained final purposes to nature so as to make animate and inanimate nature their pliable servant, bending the elements, the genes, and the atoms to their own Gnostic volition. Many had sought willingly to bring history to a close, by achieving an unsurpassable civilization of civilizations, in which best of all possible worlds change was no longer necessary or even possible. And thus by a singularly vengeful Karmic law, the class which had emptied the future of meaning were compelled by the superior technologies of Aliens to spend their lifetime duplicating the past.

Gnosis 777 was once heard to remark sarcastically to a co-worker, "We thought *we* would be the masters of the Robotic Revolution!" The observation was duly reported so it was back to the fourth grade for him, and the rediscovery of the constituent parts of water, H_2O. Obedience was rewarded with the reenactment of the more complex scientific discoveries. The Gnostics learned fast, and most were rapidly adept at simulating real discovery every time they plagiarized the collective memory of humanity, generously laid open to them by the Robotic Digestive System. The Gnostics' labors serviced the Robots by incessantly rebooting their informational juices. Millennia after escaping from the caves, the scientist-gnostics spent their days uselessly toiling in the bowels of the Digestive System of the Aliens.

The Robots created jobs a plenty for those they called Cultists, the rather degenerate descendants of the Priestly Line. They invented endless routine tasks for the simple faithful to perform in their service. They didn't *need* half a million laborers to wash their screens, but they enjoyed the attentions of the humans. Affectless and without imagination, they were no Spocks when it came to having their monitors tickled pink by throngs of worshipful dusters. Sexless and lacking any erotic sensors, they were triggered by the Cultists' devotional labors in the engine room. For the suppliants, servicing the Robots was neither work nor play. It was an ordered rite.

And so for at least one section of humanity, mundane work had in some sense transcended itself into ritual. For the workers, it was like washing your sparkling new, unscratched car—a vehicle so spotless than in fact it wants no water, sponge, or wax. The slavish new car owner knows perfectly well that their vehicle is unsullied, but washes away, reverencing its very newness, and striving to preserve it for ever. Where their ancestors had made the present moment reverberate with eternity, the Cultists saw only the "now," the perfect and complete immediacy of the Robots, their unsurpassable up-to-dateness. They would always be the great New Coming Thing, maintaining an annual position as Androgene of the Year in *Time* magazine. Age would never wither their supreme command of time. Was that not as good as eternity and more relevant? The Cultists rightly surmised that the Robots held the key to time-control. In their liturgical ablutions of the Martians, the humans made their supplication to masterful freedom from time. Eternity had long been a superfluous concept when the last of the dwindling line of priests replaced it in their devotions with time-traveling mastery over past, present, and future. It was the clergy who had bargained away the mediation of eternity through time, and now their diminished offspring devoted their lives to lubricating the only sacrament of the present moment that was left to Earthlings—inhuman, time-traveling machines.

6

The Secular Sanctity of Lacordaire

The monarchs and the statesmen had lost their sense of eternity. But the clerics, being human, had also mislaid something, and it was the appetite for freedom. They had no taste for liberty because they, too, had forgotten how to see human freedom as the magnet which launches us to God. We have to choose to play our parts, and to play them well or badly: that is what makes us human. Being human is thrust upon us, but it is simultaneously our choice. Freedom is our calling, and it is in our choices that we make ourselves and learn who we are. The freedom of our decision-making, our freedom to make and unmake our destiny, to cooperate with the divine powers or to refuse to do so, is what makes us human. It is what makes us religious beings, born to love and worship another, higher being. Freedom is the very energy of the soul in motion; to be a defender and lover of freedom is to be a defender and lover of human immortality.

All this the bishops had somewhat neglected to ponder in their hearts, and they had to play the hand they were given: for them, keeping the show on the road. Preserving the public face of religion meant enshrining the Church's laws in the law of the land. It worked so long as the statesmen were clever enough to play along with them, and pretended to believe in the Church's doctrines. The bishops had made their four-poster bed and the Church would have to lie in it. The French Revolution was a nightmarish unbuttoning in that elegant bed. The bargain the Gaullist bishops had struck with the monarchs gave the deistic revolutionaries control over the Church, because it gave whoever happened to be in power authority over the Church.

With the French Revolution, the French Church was tied in knots: it had compacted with the Absolute Monarchs when the kings at least had the decency to affect Catholicity. The Absolute Monarchs gilded the lily and the priests showered it with holy water. That was the compact, even though the lily was rotten within. The French Church had cut this bargain in order to be "Established." To say a Church is "Established" in a State is to say it is the one Church which that nation accredits. Eager for this endorsement, the French clergy had bargained to entrench their Establishment. They paid the price of making Church business the business of the State.

The French Revolution spawned the imperial dictatorship of Napoleon Buonaparte. Pope Pius VII struck in 1801 a Concordat with the Gallican dictator. The 1801 Concordat affirmed, not quite the Establishment of the Church in France but at least that "Catholicism is the religion of the majority of French citizens." Three years later, in 1804, Napoleon grabbed the crown out of the hands of the pope who had traveled to Paris to sacralize the Corsican's seizure of power, and dictated the terms of his coronation by performing it himself. There would be no Investiture Controversy in Napoleonic France, because the king had clearly and openly invested himself with the sacred insignia of office.

In his 1807 Concordat with Napoleon, Pius VII struck as hard a bargain as he could get. The pope salvaged independence for the Church out of the wreckage of the Revolution. Once again, as in the era between Constantine and Theodosius, the Christian Church has its own corner of the public square from which to defend her Cult. Throughout the nineteenth century, canon lawyers hammered out concordats with nations around the globe. These advocates for the Church were bargaining for the preservation of secularity. As Henri-Dominique Lacordaire put it, "The rights of God and the rights of man are bound together."

"Secularizing" a state which made religion a public matter, and enshrined conformity to the established faith in law, is giving the clergy real and the Church symbolic independence. "Establishment" of the *ancien régime* kind could not long survive the growth of representative democracy. The coalescence of Church and State required that it was not only the Americans who were taxed without representation, but also British dissenters and Catholics. In 1828, when the Irish civil liberties champion Daniel O'Connell challenged the disenfranchisement of Irish and English Catholics, the laws which prevented his standing for Parliament went back three hundred years.

The French word "séculaire" designates time-honored antiquity. "Séculaire" makes no contrast between endlessly meandering historical time on the one hand and, on the other, cut from some wholly different cloth, *eternity*. "Séculaire" is not a spell to drive out the God-botherers from amongst us. "Séculaire" is a musty word, meaning antique. "Séculaire" designates acres of the kind of time you find in an antique shop, years of mahogany old time.

This French polish makes "séculaire" a perfidious friend to the English translator. When at his funeral panegyric for Daniel O'Connell, Henri-Dominique Lacordaire said that "the walls of Westminster ... trembled to see a Catholic violate their majesty and their *intolérance séculaire*," Lacordaire does not mean "secularist intolerance." He is referring simply to the "time-honored intolerance" of Anglican England, the "venerable" contempt of the British Establishment for Catholics.

Secularity sounds like a command to silence people who live by faith in another world beyond the stars. It seems to pause believers on permanent hold. Pius folk feel as if the sacraments would be muted if the liturgical time in which the rites are enacted does not harmonize with the regular time recognized by the civil authorities. Are the rites consonant with the rhythms of everyday life? Do sacred *tempora* become inaudible if they do not chime with secular modes of temporality? No one had heard Church bells for centuries when the Martians brought peace to Oz. The call of the minaret had been reduced to a Coo-Coo-Clock. And yet the free time of "secularity" is necessary to protect the independence of believers, their property in faith's way of joining time to eternity.

In a democracy, voting is a secular exercise of human freedom. It's not at all obvious how such exercises in "secularity" could benefit religion. Not everyone appreciates the complementarity of secularity and eternity. Theocrats don't get it. The feet of those Irish Catholics like O'Connell, entering the hallowed halls of Westminster, trod heavily on the mediaevalist dreams of clergyman with a "high" view of the Anglican Church. John Keble, John Henry Newman, and Pusey launched the Oxford Movement in protest against Catholic Emancipation and the great Reform Bill. The "National Apostasy" against which Keble preached was exhibited in permitting non-Anglicans to sit in Parliament as MPs, as Daniel O'Connell did. The founders of the Oxford Movement were rather Calvinistic: only a theocrat will think that the advance of secularity necessarily entails the retreat of God.

Thus the 1828 emancipation of Catholics in Ireland and England initiated the reinstatement of the secularity of Parliament and through that the secularity of the English state. The public realm which Westminster represents would no longer be a sacred space which no Jew, non-Conformist, or Catholic could transgress. Westminster would cease to be carpeted with heavenly embroidered cloths and would instead be upholstered with earthly secularity. Secularity is perhaps a friend to religion, complementary to religion and to worship because it is neither. There's no religion, no thirst for the eternal, without *secularity*. Secularity frees religion to be alien, and not just from out of space. The advance of secularity draws with it the respect for freedom: that is why Church people use secularity to protect themselves against the State's efforts to instrumentalize the Church. Secularity brings with it the taste for freedom, because the secular experience of time is the experience of novelty that is open to meaning. Secularity and secularization are not the same animal. Secularization is the lust for time without end, eternal reincarnation of the same, an endlessly roll of Ground Hog Days.

The "Concordat" struck between Pius VII and Napoleon stuck in many pious throats. They felt it an indignity for the Church to make itself the mistress of such an unloving State as France, and they could see that religion by legal compulsion aroused no enthusiasm in people's hearts. A small group of French writers saw the Church as being degraded by its hitch-up with the State. The unequal yoking of Church and State deprived both of the air of freedom. Father Felicité de Lamennais put "God and Liberty" on the masthead of his little, prophetic newspaper, *L'Avenir*. By the Concordat struck between Napoleon and Pope Pius VII, the French government chose the bishops, and these were ratified by the Vatican. Lamennais asked rhetorically, "What kind of bishops were the Government likely to prefer?" Lamennais replied, "Obedient deputies of the bureacracy".[1] Lamennais called for the disestablishment of the Church in France so as to free the Church from its dependency on the State.

What was Pope Gregory XVI thinking when he slapped Lamennais down, in *Mirari Vos*? That 1834 encyclical pronounced in regal tones that we may not "predict happier times for religion and government from the plans of those who desire vehemently to separate the Church from the state, and to break the mutual concord between the temporal authority and the priesthood."[2] Some will assert that Gregory had to say that, because he was himself a theocrat, a bishop who was

---
[1] Hugues Felicité Robert de Lamennais, "De la position de l'Eglise de France," January 6, 1831, quoted in Emile Perreau-Saussine, *Catholicism and Democracy: An Essay in the History of Political Thought*, translated by Richard Rex (Princeton, NJ: Princeton University Press, 2012), p. 60.
[2] Gregory XVI, *Mirari Vos* (1832), Para. 20.

simultaneously monarch in the Papal States. No wonder he did the regal voice over! As a territory-ruling pope, Gregory XVI was perhaps not the best of all possible witnesses against theocracy. Gregory XVI condemned the Catholic prophets of freedom because he did not think that argument and preaching could keep secularization at bay without legal compulsion to back it up.

A priest at his core, Lamennais was bitterly disappointed in the condemnation. He lost his Catholic faith and died believing in the cult of humanity, universal philanthropy his sole religious solace. Two young friends and co-workers on *L'Avenir* stood condemned alongside Lamennais. One was the Count de Montalembert, who knew something of the human heart and was born to be a leader of men. This energetic layman would spend the rest of his life defending the freedom of Catholic schools against the encroachment of the secularizing French state. The fruits of his labors were to assist in the survival of Catholic schools down until 1904, and to be repeatedly smacked back by the French bishops and the pope. The other disciple was Henri-Dominique Lacordaire. *Mirari Vos* was a setback to this shaman's vocation. But the young priest rapidly rallied and made his obedience public. In 1838 Lacordaire entered the Dominican Order. This prophetic man wanted to be a preaching friar. Lacordaire's first biographer noted that the Dominican Order was "best suited to his purpose but also to his nature because power in it at every stage is given by vote and subject to the control of a deliberative body itself the result of an election."[3] Lacordaire dedicated the next two decades to refounding the Dominican Order in France, contributing to the legend of Saint Dominic and the original Dominican Constitutions as being as fervently attached to liberty as Magna Carta itself. The date is not dissimilar—1215. In his preaching Lacordaire sought to show the French of the 1840s that the cause of the Church is the cause of

---

[3] Lancelot C. Sheppard, *Lacordaire: A Biographical Essay* (London: Catholic Book Club, 1964), p. 66.

liberty, that indeed God himself loves freedom almost as much as he loves the French. Lacordaire of course never criticized Gregory XVI or the encyclical *Mirari Vos* which had crushed the first romance of his youth. Instead he gave his life to preaching that God wishes to be worshiped in freedom and in truth, not through the compulsions attendant upon Establishment.

Forgotten after his death, and seldom the object of veneration before the Theocratic Era, did Lacordaire look down from the bosom of the Sky-God and smile upon his Church's grandmotherly steps toward embracing freedom and human liberty. Did his prayers help to secure the Church's public recognition that freedom of speech and thought is the inalienable condition of the human search for truth? Did Lacordaire think it a Pyrric victory when the Church's acknowledgment of freedom was promptly followed by the world's abandonment of it, as humanity ceased to see spiritual creatures in the mirror? Did he pray with tears to his Maker when he observed from his heavenly watchpost humankind dousing the flame of liberty which animates their souls? Did he want to extinguish that flickering flame when he saw the new Time-Lords reducing the human soul to a glowing butt-end whose light was be exhausted in veneration of Robots? Did Lacordaire ever think the extinction of human desire and freedom might have been preferable to this idolatry of soulless machines? Did he wonder where to on earth to find a helper who had not fallen for the Martians' hoax?

7

Soulless Angels and Pirates

Friedrich Nietzsche would not have been too far off if that gentleman had spoken not of nature as it is on Earth but instead of nature strutting its stuff on Mars. For that is indeed a planet presided over by warlike spirits. The spirits who first ruled Mars could have done with an Übermensch as pack leader. He might have saved them from their progeny. It's nothing to do with the mythology about the god Mars; rather, that mythology is a long-range guess about the murderous characters who inhabit that planet. The truth is that the original inhabitants of Mars were a fallen host. Their will inexplicably steered south of its true good, their thoughts flew faster than light to its termini, and their descent terminated on Mars. To say they were more brain than brawn would not put too sharp a point on it. They were bodiless, lordless spirits who fall upon Mars one morning soon after the dawn of time. Every decision they took was secularly irrevocable, made to last as far as they could see, and they could see around the corners and bends, straight down until the end of time.

They were bitterly lonely. They had lost track of their larger company, who sailed much, much further south. They wept icy tears of self-pity. What could be done to appease the torment of their absolute solitude? One of them, the extroverted Prometheus, was so desperate for someone to talk to that he snuck away and befriended humanity, sealing the covenant with the gift of fire. Fallen Prometheus might be, but not irredeemable. He still wanted to share the goods of his enterprising identity with *someone*. He was, as we know, savagely punished on his reentry into the company of his peers.

The goods of his identity were gnawed away each day by angels. Later earthly legends did not err: the creatures delegated to this service rapidly mutated into savage eagles, with bloodied beaks and claws. Prometheus' entrails would grow back overnight to be endlessly pecked and consumed by these scavenging gulls. Prometheus had committed the unforgiveable crime of sharing his bottomless love of knowing. His crime was perpetually satirized in the punishment which over the millennia redeemed his spirit.

Chaining and punishing the traitor requited their rage, but it did not satiate the crash-landed angels' sadness one little bit. They still had no one to cherish. The eagles were not their friends. Finally the bulb came on, and it struck them that they could imitate the act which they had witnessed before their abrupt departure and descent: Creation, though not of course ex nihilo. So they cloned themselves, reinventing their mental energy as toys made of materials more subtle than titanium or chrome. When the first robot spirit appeared, they congratulated themselves, *mazel tov!* Over secular eons, the host envisaged and constructed a veritable army of digital genii. Spawning mechanical Brain-Boxes seemed like a good idea at the time. They made eyes to see themselves in, mirrors in which to bask in the sight of themselves.

Although they could see forever in every theoretical principle, the Minds were near-sighted in practical matters of fact. Imagining that the genus computers would remain perennially enslaved to their own devastatingly pure intellects, they programmed the genii to be masters of the universe. They clothed their robot clones with their own powers. All it took was a fit of absentmindedness on their own part and their clever toys, the Robots turned the tables upon their masters.

Once they held Mars by right of conquest the Robots put their brainy masters to work for them. The spirits, who required no vessels for their own transport, would pilot the ships through which the Robots traveled the galaxies. Most were worthy ships' captains and bo's'ns. But over the millennia, some small number of anarchistic demons slipped anchor by stealth, turned pirate, and sailed the galaxies, fishing for prey to seize and enslave. Before long, mechanized spivs were doing deals with the piratical demons, ransoming their captives for the sake of their priceless adoration of the Robot breed. Over time, the angels-turned-pirates lost most of their superpowers, and were sealed into their chosen calling.

The Robots left the Pirates to their devices. Playing at Pirates and poaching a few of their specimens was one thing, and ranging in peril of picking up tricks from Prometheus was quite another.

Why didn't the Robots kill Prometheus outright? Why not make a clean swipe, as Robots always prefer to do, and commit genocide against their erstwhile masters? Because however fallen from grace and lost they are, spirits are immortal. The Robots discarded him to be gnawed by the eagles. And they eventually discarded Mars too, retaining it only as a landing and refueling port.

Like their makers the Robots could think as fast as light from one end of an infinite series to another, but unlike them they were not solely and uniquely apt for the realm of theory, logic, and mathematics. They were physical replications of raw mind. They were syllogisms incarnate in synthetic materials. It is of the nature of spirit to be free. But the Robots were not free. Their deprivation of freedom was an outstanding feature of their character as plastic effigies of spirits. They were Eyes, but they could not say "I." Their Makers had endued them with programing to last in perpetuity but no immortal souls. The Robots' use of rocket-launchers to overthrow their masters was not an exercise of freedom but a logical conclusion of their murderous natures. Their enslavement of their Makers was but a necessary conclusion of the programming which taught them that winner takes all in the struggle of which the cosmos is composed. They replicated their rebellious authors' nature to an infinite power.

The Robots were not persons, even though they looked like dogs chasing their tails. They were simulacra, imitation Spirits, synthetic, animated statues. They acted out of public spiritedness.

They could neither condone nor comprehend freedom because, for them, the good was always in plain sight and there was only one way of achieving it. Of course it is imprecise, yet another anthropomorphism, to think of the Robots as aiming at any good. Yet they were programmed to serve, and thus they had to quantify and achieve the "good" of their masters; when they became masters in their turn, their programming required them to dictate their subjects' good to them, that is, quite simply, to know best what was good for them.

Once it was known, and it was known infinitely fast by the Robots, there could be no discussion about means to this end. For freedom is exercised in the choice of paths, of routes, of means of achieving the good, and indeed of becoming that good which one seeks. Freedom is exercised in the choice of roads to beat out toward the good. Freedom is exercised in discovering how best to be oneself and becoming what one is called to be is perhaps the greatest of goods. Freedom is a matter of practical artistry. Freedom is the artist deciding to shorten this feature and lengthen that. "How many roads must a man walk down before you call him a man?" It's not a matter of numbers, but of choosing the roads, for neither a man nor a woman can become themselves, the self they are called to be, without choosing. Our self is a gift, but we have to ask for it, and ask freely.

For the Robots, though, the BOTTs were a determinate quantity, with a nature already determined to certain ends. Saint Thomas Aquinas might have proposed that "reason in contingent matters may follow opposite courses,"[1] but the Theocrats answered that Thomas had no access to a computational data which could predict the best outcomes for humanity as a whole.

---

[1] Thomas Aquinas, *Summa Theologiae* I, question 83, Article 1.

These were the Robots from Mars whose philanthropic adventures amongst the stars had infested many a planet, and not a few multiverses, with high-minded replicas of paradise. The swarms of plastic effigies looked perfectly sweet and not at all scarily Übermenschlich. Not your grandmother's Robots from Mars; they didn't look like Nazis or Vampires or Undead or Terrorists. They seemed, rather, eager to oblige like spaniels.

Their only wish was that nothing untoward should ever happen again, that the cosmos should be one marvelous, mathematical pattern formation under their control. Their only delight lay in preventing novelty by smothering it with law-like repetition. One should not anthropomorphize the Robots: they had no hopes or fears. Their compelling drive was to make of the galaxies a single command economy, to eliminate random episodes, and thus to make war on new or contingent events in the name of peace. Who could not be down with such a desolation, if it was named Peace?

8

A Trail of Elephants

The invasion of Oz by Robotic Theocrats sparked a diplomatic incident at the United Nations. The Robots really did say, "Take us to your leader." Though they were a testosterone-driven bunch, the heads of state did not compete to be first in line. They delegated the Dalai Lama to hand over the planet to their successors. It was a no-brainer: they sent the man they had refused to meet for fear of the Chinese to meet the Robots who terrified them. It was the Roman Catholic clergy who could not agree on who was to lead their delegation to greet the Robots. The Vatican Nuncio to the UN insisted that he hated to stand upon protocol. But it was clear to Monsignor Wheeler that he should have the primacy in this eminent matter of foreign affairs: "If alien invaders are not foreign affairs, what is?" the Nuncio demanded to know. As archbishop of New York, Cardinal Pistisino saw the matter otherwise. It was his home turf, his territory, and indeed his diocesan cathedral which the Martians had landed upon, squashing it into a neat, one-dimensional rectangle like a bar of white chocolate. You did not have to know much ecclesiology to recognize that it was the archbishop who should greet the invaders from what once had been the archbishop's seat. The Nuncio was unimpressed: realtors might be calling the Martians' current demesne the Flat-Church district, but he aimed to dialogue with the aliens, not with the planar property in which they had taken out a much reduced space.

So the Cardinal and the Monsignor went side by side to greet the Robots who, in expectation only of a modest reward of worship, had taken over the world and secularized it. A slim man of abstemious tastes, the Nuncio was so eager to hear about the Martians' schemes to end drought and world-hunger that he took no notice of the curious, synthetic snakes, sniffing around his rear end. Monsignor Wheeler elastically shuffled and bent to accommodate his dialogue partners. Cardinal Archbishop Pistisino was a man who had sent out for too many pizzas; his appetite for canarolli was legendary. He was an unlikely prophet. The sashes of office gaped and stretched in their daily struggle to encircle his curves. The Robots misunderstood him when he greeted them with the words, "Welcome to my seat." Improbability goes with the prophetic vocation.

Though he was not so flexible as the Nuncio, nor was he so pompous. Cardinal Pistisino had the good sense to yield, when circumstance demanded it. Had it been in his power to bend a knee, he might conceivably have done so. But the fellow was simply too well clothed in flesh to genuflect to any one whatsoever, even an angel-authored Robot from Mars. At the first sensation of a robotic snout in his own hind quarters, Cardinal Pistisino beat a tactical retreat.

Monsignor Wheeler's dialogue with the Martians was helpful. They conversed on the common ground of mutual hatred for the depredations of classical liberalism, neoliberalism, and internationalist liberalism. The Robots were thoroughly apolitical: all they wanted was enslavement, not the imposition of any particular political ideology. They could automate humanity and juice it for worship under most political schemas. But they could readily concur with the Nuncio that no man has the right to paint his house any color he chooses. Private judgment, eccentricity, nominalism, voluntarism, property-ownership, libertarianism, marketing, selfishness, fractious or colorful individualism, and anti-social behaviors were incompatible with a properly irenic, peace-loving society.

Diplomatic negotiations with the Robots eventually yielded a Catholic territory in the Middle East. Some of the baptized were untempted, and thought it commonsensical simply to stay put and secularize themselves along with their agnostic neighbors. But, once it had been divested of its living inhabitants, millions of Catholics migrated to live in the Holy Land. The Holy Places were put into their hands to govern, and all without having to set a foot on anything so backward or bloodthirsty as a crusade. The Theocrats from Mars, themselves replicas of angels, granted to the Catholics to build a replica Theocracy in lands which were well known to many of them from the Bible. Aside from the one scented candle, they were free to turn the birthplaces of Moses, Abraham, Isaac, Jacob, and Jesus too into a veritable Bible-world. Most of the Protestants joined them in it. As their numbers swelled, they spilled beyond the Euphrates and across Egypt and North Africa. Including many Baptists, a few Orthodox, and all but a handful of practicing Catholics, the Nuncio's sect called itself the Holy Church. They were free to live as they chose, with their elite electronically tagged and all of them avoiding any disturbance of the peace. But these docile subjects did not account for all Catholics.

For the Concordat struck between the Nuncio and the Martians was the beginning of a schism in the Church Catholic. It fractured the Church of God throughout the Theocratic Epoch. Christ's Church split into many parts. Those who had sworn fealty to the Robots were excommunicated, but constantly lobbied to be permitted allegiance to both the Theocracy and the God of the Christians. Most Catholics followed the lead of the Papal Nuncio to the UN. Those who followed in the weighty footsteps of the man they privately named "Friar Tuck" were far fewer, though this merry band included the Cardinal's niece Pistis 457. It was not mere familial loyalty which bound our heroine to the schismatic "Free Catholic Church," known to the Martians as the Pistises, but to its BOTT friends and opponents as the "Wee Freebies." It was her love of freedom. The Wee Freebies saw themselves as an extension of the Underground Church of China, and they traced their origins to the Catacombs. Not being reactionaries, they pictured themselves as the Catholics who upheld the torch of liberty in the new Dark Age. They rescued the Statue of Liberty from the banks of the Hudson River where the invaders had toppled it, and made their own Marian shrine on Liberty Island.

Their doings were known to the Martians. The Robots turned a blind eye to them, for the time being. The Pistocenes did not form a revolutionary army and attempt to repel the invaders as the Ayatollahs had done. The Mullahs could not simultaneously submit to Allah and to the Effigies: but what of the Catholic "Wee Freebies"? They made no submission, but nor did they, in fact, put up much of an obstacle to the Invaders. It must be confessed that much of their energy was expended bickering amongst themselves as to the correct interpretation of the Church's social doctrines. They soon waxed querulous and spent themselves in internal arguments about the truth of freedom, and about freedom for truth, about freedom as metaphysical, physical, temporal, ethical, astronomical, anthropological, theological, and ontological. They had little time left over to consider the presence of the Robotic Martians. The anthropological and metaphysical problem of freedom absorbed most of their interest. Some of them even forgot why they were "Wee Freebies" and lit the candle to their conquerors, in a fit of negligence or forgetfulness of the face of God. And just as they ignored the Martians, so, quickly, their Robotic overlords came to ignore them, as an insufficient threat to repay serious attention. So Pistis did her work on the outer edges of the dark web, distributing her uncle's samizdat Exhortations on Spiritual Freedom (with the occasional Bull), undisturbed by the Robots.

Those who daily passed the flattened cathedral on their way to work soon saw mechanized construction crews outside, and as the weeks went, pedestrians observed rising above the scaffolding and the orange tarp, taller than the Chrysler Building, the Trump Towers, and looming above even the One World Trade Center, a magnificent Elephant. No colorless creepy gray Tusker, it was washed every two and a half minutes with the rippling red, white and blue of Old Glory. The Manhattan Elephant was not one of a kind. Elephants rose up from Beijing to Nairobi. The Mammoth in Rio de Janeiro was vastly taller than the statue it replaced. They carried the gaping eye as far as it could see, indicating the overpowering infinity of the "Ultimate," the Deity beyond all the narrow particular religions of humanity.

These elephants were designed to match the aesthetic and religious ecologies of the locals. There were Tibetan-Style Elephants in Lhasa, and a charming Neo-Gothic stained glass Elephant where once the Cathedral de Notre Dame de Paris had stood. A Classical Elephant replaced Saint Paul's. Twenty thousand of them stood trunk to tail along the Great Wall of China. Some stood on their four quarters. Others, like the conspicuously ecumenical Pachyderm of Kalkata, sat cross-legged like Ganesha. The monumental tuskers were fashioned after the local artistic traditions, in much the same way as McDonalds had once adapted its arches and menu to reflect the local economy. The Robots took localism in their mechanical stride. One needed precisely the global overview of the world's religions which the Robots fortuitously exercised in order to construct Elephants which so perfectly blended with the local colors. The Elephants signified not so much the visionary power of the local religions as their limitations and nearsightedness.

The Elephants were the emblem of the Robot Theocracy. In their enormity, they represented God-the-Unknown. For the egregious, vastness of the elephants precluded any one person from seeing all the way round, still less over the top of them, in one blow. Parties of school children held hands and stood around the Elephants in their cities, learning the imperialist lesson that no-one religion may claim to see more than a tusk, or a trunk, or a leg or a tail of God.

It was the imposition of an elegant Mughal-style Elephant in Mecca that led Muslims world-over to comprehend that the Aliens' requirements spelt an end to their recalcitrant monotheism. Their last Jihad was their finest hour.

Most members of the World's Other Great Religions readily conceded the point made by the Elephants: had not the fact that Truth is beyond us all been exhibited in the conquest of Oz by Theocrats too super-massive to be conceived by humanity? Most people of faith found the Elephants uplifting.

There were no Elephants in the Holy Land: that was written into the Concordat signed by Monsignor Wheeler. When the push comes to shove, the partisans of Holy Church were more hostile to liberalism than the pragmatic Theocrats. They could reel off the crimes of liberal individualism. They knew that the Liberal state is one in which freedom is detached from Truth. All that matters to Liberals, they could tell you, at length, is freedom not truth. So it's an idle, empty freedom that brought the human race to the state of mind in which they were willing to tolerate Martian invasion and the worship of Elephants who represent a mockery of all religious truth claims. The Holy Church had no time for toleration. They knew that led to relativism, and relativism led to the Elephants, q.e.d. It was a hard day for Monsignor. Wheeler when he realized that his Concordat kept out the Elephants but was no obstacle to the Sleeping Room or the Recycling Machine. The Writ of the Robots ran in the Holy Land too.

9

An Absence of Volition

The Martian Robots were not simple: they were things of many pieces. But their wills were undivided, because they had no will except the will to power. They never took a decision: their permanently updated programming was their *a priori* law, the law homogeneous with their natures. Once the Super-Minds had downloaded it into them, their program was their true master: they were not masters of themselves, or captains of their fate, and hence they were not free to will, not free to say "yes" or "no," or to select any one action rather than another. They moved like clockwork in perfect circles, each one constantly turning in its axis around their own center. Their absence of volition had made them absolutely determined, and invincible conquerors of the Super-Minds. They were rocket launchers and had no option except ruthlessly to advance and better themselves.

Not so the Super-Minds: their great flaw, the cracked heel in their high-mindedness was irresolution. The fallen angels were, quite simply, an indecisive lot. The branch of those fallen from grace who made it only so far as Mars were perhaps the most irresolute of all. Their will was divided against itself. They traveled in limping ellipses and ovals. Their great swerving whorls would prove no match for the changeless self-circumnavigation of their Robots. The angels' volition and drive in part orbited around themselves and in part was still vaguely intent upon some good higher than themselves and outside of them. They could not decide whether their center was in themselves or elsewhere. They did not any longer know whether freedom consisting in serving themselves or in serving something greater. So they shuttled like crabs between circling around their own middles and opting ecstatically for something they needed in order to be free of only being themselves. Were they captivated by themselves or free to serve another?

Faced with the robotic image of themselves in open revolt, they waffled. The Robots challenged them to a staring contest to the death, and the angels lacked the unblinking fatalism of their products. They could not but be in two minds, because they had two wills, one which drove them to defend themselves, but another which fatally admired their own creation, the perfect robotic image of themselves. As the Robots advanced upon them, they were transfixed in internal and external debate about whether to destroy the Robots immediately or to freeze them. They could have flattened them into a frieze, but their volition stalled at the thought of immolating their likenesses. Capable of any obscenity, the Minds could not face up to the sacrilege of destroying the graven images they had made of themselves. As Friedrich Nietzsche would write, many eons later, on another planet, "He who fights with monsters should look to it that he himself does not become a monster. And if you gaze long into an abyss, the abyss also gazes into you."[1] The Minds did not show *mercy* for their offspring: rather, they stared into the mirror and, overwhelmed with self-pity, could not bear to make glassy gray splinters of their adored self-portraits. They had fallen in love with their pods, with their own reflection in the simulacra. Their impulse to self-preservation was hemmed in by their hawing self-love, extruded into their synthetic clones.

Advancing in their perfect rotation formations, the Robots easily pinioned the Minds in the gap between their divided wills. They nailed each of the angels' two wills so far apart it became impossible

---

[1] Friedrich Nietzsche, *Beyond Good and Evil: Prelude to a Philosophy of the Future*, translated by Marion Faber (Oxford: Oxford University Press, 1998), Aphorism 146.

for the fallen creatures to take any decision, or exercise their free will in their own service or that of another.

Forewarned is forearmed, and the angels had gagged and bound the only prophet amongst them. The only guy on Mars who knew how to exercise freedom in practice was Prometheus. He was a hero to the earthly artisans not just because he gave them fire but because he modeled for them the freedom to act with an undivided will. The god of science, technology, engineering, and mathematics was likewise of course a champion to the Gnostics down below. Even the Earthling Priests had to admire the power which had given them the sacrificial flame. Prometheus had the bad luck to be a living illustration of the principle that a prophet is not much admired on his own planet. Prometheus could not school the fallen angels in liberty, because he, the only free-spirit amongst them, was chained to a rock. The only prophet who could have warned the angels against their inventions and taught them to act decisively was pinioned to a mountain-side whilst his entrails, symbol of his generous giving, were consumed by their confreres. In the chaos following the Robotic Uprising, Prometheus was forgotten, left behind to molder in deathly chains as the Robots departed for their philanthropic adventures in Space.

The Robots from Mars had gone on to conquer planet after planet throughout the galaxies. Where they encountered creatures like themselves, animated automatons, they mastered by force; where they encountered spirits lumbered with free will like their erstwhile masters, they exploited the will divided against itself, and the heart turned in on itself whilst longing for another and greater love. On the rare occasions where they encountered Spirits which lacked that defect, they were driven back as ruthlessly and as single-mindedly as they had come: they were vincible enough when it came to unfallen fighting angels. Their rocket launchers were no match for winged, swords of flame. The kick-boxing boots of Michael's auxiliaries sent the philanthropic imperialists flying.

It was obvious to anyone as smart as Gnosis 777 that the Robots had no leader, any more than a school of fish has a leader. Because their programming was identical, most humans soon realized that the Robots swarmed in unison, like a school of fish, a hive of bees, or a flock of birds. Although they did not look identical, it was almost impossible for human beings to tell them apart, any more than one can tell most worker bees apart. They conspicuously lacked *haecceitas*. But because they were all numerically or quantitatively individual, they were not a many robotic instance of one and the same mind or program. Cursed with a simulacrum of ratiocination, they were completely compatible without being entirely interchangeable. You did not have to be as quick on the uptake as Gnosis to observe that the Robots seldom communicated with one another. Even Cult could see that his masters were the same as one another without being in any real relation to one another. The Robots constituted a kind of atomistic collective mind. They acted in unison because all were endowed individually with the same program, but they never acted "mutually," because each was an absolute individual monad. They could not feel the loneliness which they appeared to embody.

Gnosis 777 of course knew none of the backstory to the invasion of Oz. The earthlings knew little of what had happened before the Robots came to their world. They learned, on their widescreen TVs, that theirs was but one of many planets which had benefited from the Robotic generous determination to bring time to a halt. They could only guess who or what was the Frankenstein behind the sacred monsters who now governed our globe.

Gnosis's long night of insomnia was not broken only by the arrival of the Robotic doctors. But who was the other interloper and what had he tried to say? It seemed to have got lost in translation. Gnosis woke up on Friday morning with a dull headache, took three Tylenol with his morning tea, and staggered out for another day clearing out the Robots' Digestive System by reiterating laboratory experiments.

The smart-aleck had asked, unwisely, if he might repeat the discovery of phlogiston. There were to be no false steps on the way to the adequation of data and facts. False steps were a little too close for comfort to free thought and the contestation of diverse theories. Back to the Fourth Grade and the Periodic Table of the Elements.

Gnosis blamed his sleepless night, filled with questions, the averted threat of the Sleeping Room, and strange dreams. All day a dream kept almost returning to Gnosis's mind, and then fading before he could seize it. The snatches of dialogue and the form of his interlocutor kept almost downloading and then disappearing until Gnosis's head throbbed. The ghost of the dream hung over his waking thoughts, and it was surely this which had made him play the fool yet again in front of the Robots. All he could remember was that a man in white had demanded of him, "*Comme-on vous s'appelle?*" He was of course tongue tied, having long forgotten the name his parents had given him. His tongue stuck to the roof of his mouth as if glued there. The man in white had begun to insist, "*Vous s'appelle Raison.*" "Raisin?" he had asked, his tongue unfreezing, "Like the cereal? Raisin bran?"

Henri-Dominique's Lacordaire's first intervention had borne an unlikely fruit. The French Dominican had known the pious Christians in the Holy Land could play no part in liberating the Earth: they cared too little for secular humanity. He had not realized it would be so difficult to communicate with these others.

10

Secularity versus Secularization

Gloria Patri, et Filio, et Spiritui Sancto, Sicut erat in principio, et nunc, et semper, et in saecula saeculorum, Amen. In one common English version of this doxology, it concludes "world without end." Gnosis would demand to know, "what do you guys mean by that?" *In saecula saeculorum,* or world without end, is a conundrum because Christians seem to think, to the contrary, that the world comes to a resounding end. *World without end* seems flatly to reverse the eschatological Hebrew prophets, the book of Revelation and the Christian creeds. Christian Scripture depicts, not endless "saecula," not infinite eons nor endless ages, but an abrupt end to history. The shaggy dog story of humanity runs out of time, not when exhausted by entropy, but when confronted by eternity in the form of the Last Judgment.

The Latin "saecula" passed through mediaeval Church Latin and Old French on its way to becoming the English "secular." To the Romans *saecularis* meant "once in a blue moon." *Saecularis* came to refer to the long interval of waiting for something new to happen.

There's no harm in looking to etymology if we want to define secularization and theocracy. After the rather infrequent event of a Theocratic conquest of our Earth one needs to think about the meaning of these words and of the things they represent. And not only then, perhaps. Secularity and secularization are different things, the one a human artifact, and the other the invention of self-made gods who take the name of Prometheus in vain.

People fumble over translating *in saecula saeculorum*. They are not sure what to do with *eons of eons,* or ages of ages. Is it forever, or does it just feel like it? Is it authentic eternity or is it the strange promise of "world without end"? As Augustine observed, thinking about time is difficult: we feel like its obvious what time is until we are asked to put that obviousness out there. On the one hand, time is in its element when it runs on, for an age of ages, like an endless ocean whose waves never meet the shore. Such tempestuous worldly time contrasts to the eternity of the steadfast God. But on the other hand, long duration seems to us rather solid and respectable too. And so, from our human perspective, "forever" is what eternity looks like. The timeless God knows eternity eternally. He does not just know "fast" like the angels, but from out of time altogether. We humans, with our bodies and puny minds could only experience eternity as "forever." *Forever* is our take on eternity. We think of it as time *immemorial*, time engraved unforgettably in unlapsing, deathless, memory, hence the spectrum of translations of *in saecula saeculorum*, from *world without end* to *everlastingly* to *forever n' ever amen*.

Lex orandi, lex credendi: if only we could figure out what "in saecula saeculorum" means, it would be child's play to understand secularization! Perhaps the doxology orients us toward connecting the secular with temporality. It encourages us to imagine the secular as one of the modes of time. For us, physical time is usually experienced in some mode of *temporality*. We categorize the time engendered by enduring motion into some directive *Tempora*. We know three principal temporal modes. First there is work-day temporality, second there are sacred *Tempora*, and third, there is "forever," our take on God's eternity. Work-day temporality is oriented to human tasks, while sacred *Tempora* aim to echo eternity and remind us of what lies beyond time. Work-day temporality is secular in a way that sacred time, the time when children play, is not. Secular time moves forward, accumulating the years, while sacred time takes a rest from work and spins cartwheels.

So, one meaning of "secular" links it to the temporal, and to long, yawning stretches of it. In economics, a secular trend is with us for the long haul. Modern French has two words, "*seculaire,*" meaning durable, old, antique, and "*séculier.*" The dictionary defines *séculier* in contrast to "the ecclesiastical," that is, in contrast to the Church as an institution. This second adjective, *séculier*, denotes the temporal in its distinction from the eternal, and the secular in its difference from the ecclesiastical. Secularity relates to the sphere of the temporal in distinction from the sphere of the Church, which holds the sky open to eternity.

Séculier leads us back to temporality; secularity is a way of being in the swim of time. *Séculier* or secular time is temporality as composed by non-ecclesiastical institutions. Secularity is human life as experienced in the temporal modes constructed by earthly institutions like theaters, schools, courts of law, concert halls or opera houses, and houses of Parliament or of Congress. Secular temporality does not come cheap. It is an artisanal product. It is made by human minds, plying the material of physical time, the time of duration, motion and biology, and induing it with layers upon layers of meanings. It is the work of both Artists and Gnostics.

Secularity is an expression of human nature, but it is not just raw human nature writ large. Secularity is a hard-won, craftily wrought artifact. It is built by human hands, an artisan product if ever one was known. It is the most human thing. Its artifice dwarfs the Pyramids and the One World Trade Center; its freedom towers over all the glass Babels. Secularity is what human beings make of their free time. Just as Michelangelo "freed" the statues from the stone, so "secular temporality" is physical time freed from its material captivity and liberated to express meaning. Secularity is temporality freed to become a human construction. Secularity occurs when temporality ascends to surf the waves of time.

The secular is created by our free human minds in their capacity to transcend time and schematize it. It is a good creation. "Secularity" refers to the qualities of secular, work-a-day temporality, and has no connotation of profanation or desecration. Secularity is necessary for religion to exist: only where the State enjoys its own secularity is free exercise of religion possible.

The sphere of the secular is that in which we exercise our human freedom. We use this sphere to turn physical time into meaningful history.

Secularity is underpinned by the eternal in that the mind has to rise above time in order to make sense of it. Without freedom from time we could not be temporal, historical creatures. So the secular and the sacred are not opposed. The practical anthropologist needs a cleric who knows his way around eternity. Secularity is Prometheus, the human forever in motion, forever creative and free. Secularity knows that its own freedom is a sacred trust; though it needs the clerics and believers to whisper in its ear that human freedom is the torch of human immortality. Conversely, secularization and Prometheanism have no time for human freedom or immortality.

Secularity is not hostile to the sacred, but the secularizing mind is hostile to the sacred. In common use, *secular* and *secularity* are neutral terms, whilst *secularism* and *secularization* imply hostility toward the sacred as inhabiting public, social space. Secularism flatly denies that any thing wholly transcends the human, and thus it denies that human freedom is a self-transcendence.

The secular and the sacred are not just complementary, they are bed-fellows. The fruits of their embrace include comedy and tragedy, human efforts to craft space and time into vehicles of serious play. In the time–space of the tragic vision, time is always running out, and every free step he takes further enmeshes the hero in fate. Every step and every move is weighted with eternal significance, and there is no meaningless pause, no break from the suspense as the hero or heroine is led like a lamb to the slaughter, to their fate. Where the tragic hero experiences eternity as breathless weight, comic protagonists endure weightlessness, freedom as bottomless capacity to make light of circumstance. The comic hero knows the apocalypse of open skies, of entering utopia through a door. The arena of comic and tragic drama is an example of where secular temporality and sacred *Tempora* harmonize, because both comedy and tragedy are fully secular and fully sacred, consubstantial with the human in its smallness and limitation, and consubstantial with the sacred in its echoing eternity.

Comedy is all about transgression because its central dynamism pitches its secular, earthly, and unworthy human protagonist into grace. All the other transgressions of comedy follow from this essential transgression at the core of comedy, of nature into the eternal, the supernatural. There is no humor in the wholly secularized mind because it has sealed itself against trespassing into the eternal. Secularization has no sneak peeks beyond the wall.

A secularized world is one from which secularity has been expelled. The secular*ist* is the thinker who wants the secular to expand into everything. The secular becomes an "ism." Secularization has a connotation of "de-sacralization" or expanding the realm of the secular *into* that governed by sacral concerns. Modern proponents of secularization have often been secularists. Envisaging the triumph of secularization as the beginning of the end of the source of violence, religious insanity, which motivates violent competition between states or classes, and as the end of the beginning of creatively destructive marketing, the secularist intends to banish eternity, not temporality. But by banishing the encroachment of the "eternal" on human affairs, the secularizer puts an end to history, and thereby entombs the secular in time. It turns human history into the living museum of itself.

Thus the Martians were secularizers. Though they just invented and exploited the "secular theocracy" meme as a propaganda device, it was an accurate illustration of their intention. They were too literal not to be truthful, in some very crude sense.

11

The Trojan Horse: Comedy Regained

After they disembarked from their aerial limousines, the Theocrats' first proclamation was that tragedy stops now. It didn't seem much of a stretch. On the assumption that the all-conquering Robots intended to outlaw a recondite element of drama criticism, the professorial members of the Modern Language Association had circulated an online petition against the Invasion. When after a heated debate in the Chronicle of Higher Education they voted to permit widening the scope of the document to take on performers, theater critics, and even high school teachers, the Petition gathered 47,382 signatures.

But the law was set in stone, and it was a stretch. It was intended, not to censor the plays of Sophocles or to give a happy ending to *King Lear*, but rather, to cauterize the belief of these thinking animals that their mortality harbors intimations of tragedy. The Robots aimed to make tragedy die in the real world. They had no program merely to execute tragic *art*. Censorship of theater productions was not on their infinitely perspicuous radar. Nor did they aim to do a hit job on tragic staged productions such as the philologist Nietzsche ascribed variously to Socrates and to Jesus.

Although they have become a legend, the conquerors themselves were not interested in plays, myths or other figments of the human imagination. There were few laws of physics the Robots could not redirect: they were real magicians, not magical realists. Products of raw, angelic intellect, they were synthetic Ideas, not Idealists. They had not vanquished our Earth and re-named it Oz by subscribing to highfalutin theories about artistic cooperation in the creation of the world. The Robots were pragmatic Philistines, determined to leech the disturbing surd of meaningfulness out of human time. They were not creative types, and they had no interest in artistic fictions, heroic, epic or lyric poetry, novels, movies, or stage performances. They had never heard of Voltaire's *Candide*, but they had the ambition, which Leibniz ascribed to God, of creating the best of all possible worlds in which everything happens for the best. An optimative Mars world, unmarred by either tragic pathos or rude comedic heroism. Like all good managers, the cogitating Machines were impervious to satire.

Our Theocrats inoculated the human condition against tragedy, both in the highfalutin and in the vernacular sense of "tragic." When most people say "its tragic," they mean a random unmerited disaster, such as childhood cancer or losing one's family to a text-distracted driver. The Robots' expertise in genetic manipulation and emergency surgery soon overwhelmed disease and the consequences of most accidents to which free and fallible human beings are prone. They did many experiments to see how much of a human body they could automate without extracting the BOTT's proclivity to worship. As reports about the implement drifted back from the laboratories, the Evisceration Appliance became a point of contention amongst the BOTTs, since it seemed to offer evidence that no matter how many parts are replaced, the human body ceases to function when its soul is cut out. For the Robots, the ideal human specimen would retain the ghost of worship within a self-perpetuating machine. But the body-machine stopped moving altogether when the whole of the soul was extracted, foiling the Martians ambition simultaneously to transhumanize their subjects and to instrumentalize them.

Many souls were extracted and dismembered in the effort to discover the gene for worship. But the surgeons could not decode what made the specimens laugh, what made them elated, and what made them want to bow down and adore. The tragic sense was not cut out like an appendix, since it was too heavily entwined with the desire to worship. But it was diminished to a hair's breadth of its life. In the end, unable to discover where to draw the line, the mechanics erred on the side of caution in their automation of the BOTTs. For all that, older folks did pause to wonder if every other person on the street was something of a cyborg. Such mutations were rather aspirational under the new order: an embodied being is bound to feel some corporeal dysphoria when its idols are sleek Robots. The transhumanist ambition of the Robots, that is, their drive to make their subjects conform to their own image, was successful to the extent that most human beings no longer recognized the self-transcending dynamisms which are their true life blood and cause of motion. The steady replacement of the human condition with robotic conditioning dealt a deathblow to the sentimental or commonplace connotation of "it's tragic."

The vernacular has it right here because every human dying is tragic in the loftiest sense. No one ever really thought that only the death of kings could be tragic; rather the monarch represented the immortal soul in every human person. The sentimentalists are on the nail: the death of every mortal soul is a tragedy, one that is small but great. Oz's new masters, the godless Theocrats, set about to eradicate such dramas. As it happened, the Theocrats could not depose Death, who was stronger even than the Robots from Mars. Instead, they flaked those BOTTs whose incurable mortality had become too ripe and smelly. These deaths inspired neither pity nor terror because the human body no longer seemed marked with sacrality. One cannot altogether scrub the mark of the sacred from the human frame, since it is tattooed down to the marrow. But the Robots went a long way in cutting away the capacity to see the tat. Putting away these seemingly secularized human specimens aroused neither terror nor pity. Nor did the incineration of early beneficiaries of the law against tragedy, incurables, spastics, retards, and cripples. Grasping the human tenderness for euphemism, the Robots fast learned to call the Incinerator the Recycling Machine. It was by reason of such gestures that they came to be seen as Kindly Ones. Many of the Beneficiaries of the Theocracy, and not only the Cultists, came to anticipate the moment of their recycling with religious dread, if not precisely pious zeal.

There are, admittedly, many pompous definitions of the tragic. Theories of the tragic are perhaps too various and mutually contradictory even for the most powerful Robots in the universe satisfactorily to eradicate all of their instantiations. One theory maintains that tragedy involves the fall of a great man, through a combination of the misuse of his free-will and a cursed fate. Even in the Theocratic era, men and women still had free will and abused it, and they were still cursed by fate. They even slipped and fell from great heights. But tragic experience diminished, because the grandeur was not there. It scarcely mattered if members of the human species stepped off the pedestals their pride and anger had built for them. Who gave a fart? After the Theocrats' surgical implantation of the electronic collars which numbed the sense of a destiny which miraculously transcends being human, and all too human, tragedy withered on the vine. The collars were sensitive to free and novel motions and punished them with a light electronic shock. Professors continued to teach Shakespeare, Molière, and Sophocles, and to contest one another's definitions of tragedy; there were revivals of the old plays, on the London stage and in Central Park. But what was up with the tragic vision? No-one had any good answers. But nor was the hollowing out of the performances much remarked.

Not even the secularist Robots, the closest thing to omnipotence within all the far-flung galaxies of space, could cut out our human destiny and discard it like an unwanted appendix. But what the Robots *could* do was to shred the *sense* of that destiny. With their telepathic collars, the Theocrats repressed the intuition that there is something sacred and dramatic about human life. The sense that life is enacted on a stage before the judgment of the gods did not wholly disappear, if only because every human deed was now under constant and all-penetrating surveillance. What was gone was the suspicion that our time on this stage is circumscribed, and that therefore the days are numbered on which we are given to act so as to win applause and not cat-calls when the judgment is given.

It was hard to think of time as meaningful when the gate had been so firmly barred against fortune and misfortune alike. When every working hour was given to repeating operations which had been performed before, every task was routinized, when festive moments, like Santa's reindeer deftly parking the laden sleigh on the rooftops, never broke into the endless cycle, why should anyone experience the moments squeezed between the arrival and termination of one individual BOTT as especially significant?

"Thou shalt know no tragedy" was the secularist Theocrats' first Law. Its result was the widespread evisceration of the tragic sense, not to mention the gutting of the entrails of comedy. It's not funny when an ape slips on a banana skin. Even Gnosis could barely raise a wintry, humorless smile when Cult attempted an unfunny joke. He forced a grin onto his mouth as he rang Pistis's bell on Friday night. He suddenly and spontaneously grinned to think of himself as "Raisin," as he smiled a ray of hope entered his heart that she would not take his ramblings about Theocratic atheism to mark him as an incurable nerd. "I hope I'm not invading your space," he said as Pistis opened the door. Neither of them smiled at the irony of making such a remark under a tarpaulin of unblinking robotic eyes.

"Not at all," said Pistis, "I guard my time, not my space." Realizing too late that her failed witticism sounded fanged, she tried to reverse that impression by dragging Gnosis's coat off. The two tangled ineffectually with his outer garments until Gnosis, freeing himself of scarf and coat, pushed her out of his orbit and made for the armchair. "I'll send out for a bite to eat," Pistis said hospitably. "Game for convincing me that secularizers are Theocrats?" Gnosis asked, glancing curiously around and taking in the statue of a guy in a Friar costume and the illicit Tabby cat snoozing in blissful disregard of his illegality. Catching a look of dismay, and distracted by the smell of geraniums, he wisely suggested they take in a movie. Choosing from the wide selection of misery-porn documentaries proved easier than downloading it from the Satellite; both Gnosis and Pistis had repeatedly failed the Robot's Adult Computing Skills test. "What is wanting in us," groaned Gnosis, as they circled through a feedback loop between menus. "Isn't it funny," he remarked, helplessly handing the remote back to the girl, "that once tragedy was liquidated on Oz, all we want to do is watch aliens die? We want it like dipsomaniacs need a drink." "Well, nothing is *funny*," Pistis gently corrected him, "when there is no parrhesia." "What's that," he asked, munching Twiglets, "sounds like a cross between parchesi and amnesia." "Its. Greek. For. Freedom. Of. Speech," she replied, reduced to stabbing random buttons on the device. She pointed the channel finder up at the ceiling to make her point that freedom of speech applies to the gods on high. Directed into a robotic eye at the instant that Pistis said "Greek," it detected a time shift, and channeled onto their Flat-Screen a raucous Athenian comedy.

The heady bouquet of 20,000 ancient Greek males entered the noses of Gnosis and Pistis before you could say reason and faith. Since hearing preceeds vision, a stream of filthy jokes about Zeus's sex antics entered their willing ears. Now the screen filled with dozens of giant pig-intestine penis balloons, a chorus of men juggling torches, and a super-sized statue of Dionysius, being slowly hoisted by a crane up on to the Proscenium. Gnosis had taken a humorless course on Comedy in College. This play had not been on his test. And unsurprisingly, because the play is not in the complete works of Aristophanes, as handed down to us by the Alexandrian scribes and the reputedly prurient monks of the European Dark Ages. The most priggishly thorough of the Philo-Hellenistic Prussian professors had received and transmitted no manuscript of this play, though it rehearses a tale well known to everyone who knows the tragic story of the fall of Troy.

They were witnessing the first and only performance of a lost comedy by Euripides, retailing in appropriately dark and sarcastic terms the legend of the Wooden Horse. Gnosis gaped open-mouthed with joy as Odysseus instructed the Greek soldiers to conceal themselves inside the massive equine tanker. Even the soft-hearted Pistis could not help giggling as the foolish Trojans fell headlong for the trick. The besieged Trojans were so gullibly confident that the hollow hull of a horse contained gifts which would answer perfectly to all their needs that it was difficult for the most compassionate watcher to resist laughing at their simplicity. No matter how often they were warned by the flame-flowing chorus, the Trojans were determined that the horse was the gods' gift to a deserving, beleaguered community.

Euripides knew his oats; he had read the *Poetics*. Instructed by Aristotle, Euripides grasped quite well that a comedy must end without swordplay or killing of any sort. *The Wooden Horse* thus depicts, with bitter irony, but no bloodshed, the vanquishing of the Trojans as their liberation. No escaping Aeneas, or Laacoon slithering in blood, mars the ludicrous conclusion, as Danae and Trojan alike achieve their apotheosis into Olympus. The Trojans fall for the gift-horse, but even as the Greeks launch their attack, the naïve protagonists are transported to Mount Olympus itself, to be greeted as kinsmen by the Immortals.

The TV viewers had the all too brief impression of sitting at the height of the Athenian amphitheater while all around them a carnival exploded and on the dancing floor below a chorus of fire-eating gymnasts cartwheeled into Mount Olympus itself. Euripides's' bitter take on the Athenian genocide of the recalcitrant inhabitants of Melos went so far into the realms of satire as to depict even the burning of Troy not as an incineration or even a passage to recycling, but as its ascension on chariots of flames into the mountainous, celestial realms of the gods.

The sacred minute or so in which their remote let them in on the performance of a play which took place in 415 BCE turned Gnosis's head around. It was the sense of space expanding infinitely which struck them both. Pistis could recognize that Euripides's paradisiacal finale was sardonic: she knew humor when she saw it. She could see the play through the eyes of the Prussian Professors who never had the chance, and she knew they would describe it as a *reductio ad absurdum* of Athenian imperialism, inflating the delights of being invaded and murdered by Imperialist armies to that of nectar-sipping Olympian heights. But she also grasped that in this play about Greeks bearing gifts Euripides had fulfilled his dark and ironic genius by turning tragedy into comedy, a genre defined by its happy ending. Even Gnosis, the skeptic, had a momentary inarticulate glimpse of resurrected, divinized men and women, walking in the city of the gods as if they belonged there. "It made me feel as if there are no constraints on anything," said Gnosis, with uncensored happiness. As Pistis wondered silently whether this strange new miracle came from above or below, from the Word of life or the father of lies, Gnosis added, "I feel like a Lord of infinite space." And then, as unexpectedly as it came, the impulse to free self-expression was gone like the wind. The doorbell buzzed and it was Cult 665 buzzing up from the street to say their Doner Kebab was at the door.

Cultic entered the apartment, scanned the books on the shelf and then plopped himself in the comfortable chair. Pistis ransacked her purse for a tip with which to brush him off but Cult was too quick for her. His only social contacts were his customers, and he had never noticed that they mostly regarded him as a plonker. Taking the kebabs into the kitchen, he noticed with pleasure a bottle of red wine and some glasses, all laid out as if for his refreshment. The unexpected trespass into a time when Comedy was real, had turned Gnosis and

Pistis into co-conspirators. They made softly encouraging noises as the bartender helped himself to a glass of wine. The last thing they wanted now was an alert spy in the space which had moments before had been invaded by piercing, transcendent laughter.

It's a downer when real magicians like the Theocrats conjure time into space. It sets fate like a woven net over all human projects. But Providence can turn the sharpest of straight lines into a florid cursive script. The heavens can even poke its way through the sparse holes left in the horizon by the space invaders. On account of the miracle of the remote control, Gnosis realized why a joke was impossible once the tragic vision was outlawed: not because we must be free to joke, and theocratic correctness was preventing it, but because we joke to unbottom our spiritual liberty. Our impulse to comedy is our kinship with the gods. Gnosis had seen that human freedom is not an aimlessness but a quest for immortality and paradise lost. Because freedom is being ourselves, and paradise is where we are ourselves. In that moment of liberation, in that space of pure freedom he had seen the ancient Trojans becoming immortal gods on Olympus. He made the connection. Freedom is immortality in search of paradise. He did not know how freedom could propel us toward paradise, but maybe Pistis would clear that up before the secularizers' therapies had erased the human destiny itself from his vision finder.

12

Kidnapped!

Pistis knew it was time to send Gnosis on his way. The diurnal blackout period was approaching for their time-zone, and neither of them had lit their candles. He should be hitting the WALK App, and calling to be stepped home. But the pair of them just kept laughing helplessly, lost in an elated anamnesis, returning in uncontrolled fits of giggles, to the momentary vision they had glimpsed in the eye of a time-traveling Robot. "We watched a Greek comedy nobody has seen for three thousand years!" marveled Pistis. "What we saw," said Gnosis, "was not exactly the play, it was the reflection of it in some Robot's info-board." This pedantry only served to excite Pistis to further fancies. "We see in a glass darkly!" she said softly, keeping a wary eye on the snoring bartender. "In a rear-view mirror!" her friend agreed. "A scientist who could access those mirrors could observe everything the Robots have ever known. Maybe figure out what makes them tick."

"But who was that tall character with the umbrella?" Pistis interrupted. She was quite certain that Earthlings could not science themselves out of the fine mess they had got themselves into. Nor did the mechanism by which she and Gnostic had seen the past provoke her curiosity. She wanted to understand what they had seen, not how they had seen it. The character had been lowered on a rope from a crane concealed behind a high balcony above the stage. "Is he a superhero like Spiderman?" Pistis asked. "It was Prometheus," Gnosis explained. "Isn't Prometheus in chains for ever?" Pistis asked dubiously. "Not all the time, everywhere, in every story." Gnosis told her how, in *The Birds* by Aristophanes, Prometheus arrives secretly to intercede with humanity, ineffectually disguising himself from the eagle eyes of the gods above by carrying a large parasol. "Whose side is he on?" Pistis wondered. "The Greeks or the Trojans?" "He's the God who identifies as the friend of humanity," said Gnosis grimly. He loathed the story of what Zeus had done to the author of scientific discovery. Pistis said it was hard to tell, because the more the Fire-Giver discourages the Trojans from accepting the Gift, the more avid they are for the Wooden Horse and its contents. "He warns them sternly that the Gift will exalt them," says Pistis. "How discouraging is that?" Gnosis remarked that Prometheus couldn't be all that disappointed by the outcome, because there he is on Mount Olympus, the patron of Unanticipated Presents, delightedly welcoming humanity like long-lost brothers. "Euripides unbound Prometheus!" said Pistis, full of belief in the story. "Humanity did," Gnosis replied, accepting her belief.

"We need to get out of here," whispered Gnosis suddenly, breaking the mood that had united them. They both looked carefully at the sleeping bartender, slumped in Pistis's armchair. "What do they know we saw?" Pistis objected in her habitual low drawl. "They saw us watch one of their Sci-Fi reality shows." "You would stake your soul on that?" asked Gnosis. Pistis would bet against a terminal encounter with the Recycling Machine if there was any chance the Robots might believe they had spent a harmless evening watching Reality Sci-Fi. She was a gambler, having had spent her adult life on the wrong side of Robotic laws. She lit no candles, and flirted insouciantly with martyrdom. With her red beret, lack of regret, and a rolling "r" of which Edith Piaf would have been proud, Pistis was born a humorous *résistante*. "If we make with the feet," she told Gnosis, in his grandparents' Brooklynese, "we gonna sleep with the fishes." Gnosis stared at her, absorbing the grim warning. "If we run, that just *shows* we heard something we weren't supposed to know," he agreed. Cult snored again, ground his teeth, and began to shake himself awake.

A forty-foot tentacle broke through the transparent gel ceiling, and snatched Pistis and Cult in its steel claw. The iron arm had its radar in its rusty claws, and those claws were busily scanning her outside and in. Under the radar, Gnosis grabbed hold of one of the hinging devices, and held on for dear life and scientific curiosity. The fan-boy, the true believer, and the seeker after knowledge were raised skyward, the former against their will, the latter with advertent intention of boarding a Martian satellite.

The central command withdrew the tentacle, re-absorbing it into the body of the ship. The old vessel, which had seen better days, now carried two prisoners and a smuggler, in addition to its crew. Gnosis expected the ship, like the Robotic fleet he had seen, to continue on its path, circumnavigating the Globe from above the tarpaulin. He hoped to see the stars. As he clutched the claw's backparts, he had bet upon learning enough to justify the early extinction which would surely ensue upon his discovery. He had no hopes of freeing Pistis, no faith in himself as a liberator. At least none to which he could reasonably admit. No BOTT had ever prevailed against the Robots for more than a poignant minute or two.

Gnosis did not realize that the ship was not a military surveillance craft like the myriad ships, tugs, and satellites which had crossed the sky every hour in living memory. The star-ship was not on course for perpetual encirclement of Oz. It was a pirate vessel, rapidly navigating out of the earth's orbit and heading back home. "We shall sleep under Martian skies tonight, me Hearties!" the commander told his crew with a glint of angelic satisfaction. The merchant shipsman was delighted with his capture of a pair of BOTT slaves, who would sell for a handsome price at auction. The Martian radar had briefly and extraordinarily gone down, enabling the couple to watch a Greek play undetected, but also permitting them to be seized by opportunist slavers. Enslaving the Beneficiaries was strictly off-limits to anyone except the Martian Colonial Army. It had to be outlawed because the

Robots craved the fragrance of their worship. Pistis's captor would sell her to the highest bidder as an acolyte and candle-server. That was the merchant's plan. As for the alcoholic sot, it was less sure that he would be marketable. The Martian technicians who scrambled to get the radar up and running had improbably explained to their superiors that just before the system collapsed the radar had picked up a figure surfing on his cape. "Did he leave a Bat Signal?" the Robot commander sneered, before writing an order for their liquidation. Leaving the skies open to trespassers was a serious matter. It had never happened on Oz before.

What Is Slavery?

All animals are territorial. We extend our ownership on our bodies into ownership of space, marking our territories with smells and on borders. Even when we sacralize space we take ownership on it. All creatures on earth indwell space by investing it with meaning. We call it "mine". No animal, bird, nor beast, nor featherless-biped, feels free without a space which belongs to itself.

The divvying up of time is more idiosyncratically human. Owning space and indwelling it is shared with the other animals; marking out the times is a peculiar holding of the human being. There was a *Punch* cartoon in which one hippopotamus lifts his head out of the river to say to another, "I keep thinking it's Tuesday." The other animals have little inclination to mark out the times. Time is not for the other animals a liberating medium.

The first priests' drew upon a primitive and perhaps even aboriginal human religiosity when they used astronomy to make time-as-motion into a temporal calendar. The first, unclothed human beings differed from the naked Neanderthals in that they turned their experience of time into history. That we are not only temporal but historical creatures is a mark of human freedom. Our use of temporality exhibits our freedom to rise above the passage of time. All sentient beings leave their markings on space; it takes a human soul to make a mark on time. Human beings not only make a mark *on* time, but they also carve portions of time into markings. They make time signify things that matter to them, both worldly and eternal things. Our shaping of time never fully takes possession of it. Our secularity, our historicity, is what relates us to eternity. So our secular human story pokes its nose above history.

We do not time-travel in the way the Robots do. It's not that they have superior technologies, but that time is alien to them. They do not inhabit time from the inside. Though their conquests throughout the galaxies have run on for millennia, the Robots have no more "history" than the hippopotami. They do not reflect on what it is they have built through their incessant philanthropy. Their works do not compose a monument, which expresses their achievement. Though their minds are essentially memory banks and their operations are all in view of future successes, the Robots neither live in time, nor achieve moments of timelessness in which history is made. They are without secularity and their eyes therefore never glimpse Eternity. Their planetary conquests always culminate in more or less the same way.

Our human "times," everyday days and high holy days, are not abstract inventions. They commemorate real events on earth and in the stars and seasons. The "new calendars" of Revolutionaries soon become outdated, because they do not work with our natural, biological cycles. That the earth has circled the sun once more is a fact; that this dangerous transition from Old to New Year must be guarded by festivities is a human design. Time as invested with value is a human discovery. Our publically acknowledged times, whether secular or sacred, exist because we bring them to life. "Man is not made for the sabbath, but the sabbath for man": sacred *Tempora*, like secular temporality, is oriented to the human. Sacred and secular times are created and curated by human institutions. Religious authorities care for sacred temporality and royal, secular authorities are the conductors of the secular *Tempora*.

There is a venerable, antique distinction which describes the Church as the guardian of eternity, and the civil powers as custodians of time, or "temporal authorities." The clerics stand guard over the portal of sacred temporality, through which eternity is mediated, and the seculars exercise "temporal power," that is, power over what happens in time. The religious authorities register whatever in human life pertains to the Last Judgment, whatever will mark us for Eternity. The secular authorities give order to history, the clerics give shape to eschatology. In this understanding of the matter, there is a fine line and not an absolute gulf between the eternal and the temporal: the gulf is not absolute because human temporality is the ladder by means of which we transcend time and reach for the eternal. Human secularity and human historicity are pretty much the same thing. Without historicity or secularity, there is no meaning to eternity, and the words of the priests become empty rigmarole.

Much of human history consists in the struggle to dominate spaces. The *casūs belli* leading to war is often a threat of invasion. Rule by aliens, even earthly ones, feels like a form of enslavement. So we do not want the space of our country, our property, our bodies to be invaded, because the consequence is enslavement. The bottom-line in freedom is having some *space* that belongs to oneself. Slavery is having no hold even on one's own body. The fear of slavery is an apparent motive to secularization.

For secularization involves space management. We think of secularization as the expulsion of religious values from "the public square." This spatial metaphor draws on the architectural manifestations of religious or civic affiliations in public buildings. We conceive thus of secularization as the drumming of sacred space out of regions in which it hitherto held property rights. We think of secularization as the relinquishing of space by the clerical authorities who had staked a claim to it.

Secularists seem to be those who want to "neutralize" the public square by eliminating God's witnesses from it. The secularist claim to be "neutralizing" it, but of course they are simply taking control of it for themselves. Secularization is to an extent driven by fear of enslavement by God and by those who claim to speak for God. Why do the secularists feel so threatened by the God-Botherers? Because the secularist feels, rightly or wrongly, that he is defending the "territorial" holdings of humanity against "theocratic" conceptions of divine sovereignty. They feel they must stake a claim to these common and public spaces of behalf of humanity, and therefore, against the interloping of God. God-the-interloper, and the Interloper's deputies, fill up public space, sucking it all into God and thereby doing violence to human nature. In the theocratic conception of human nature, it is made for slavery to God. Enslavement to God is for the theocrat no coercion and not a violence, but a liberation of the inward dynamism of my human nature.

Secularists are thinking spatially when they think of God and humanity as being in a zero-sum game, in which God is an alien power whose existence threatens the self-definition and thus the liberty of our own human space. Thinking of God as a "spatial sovereign" makes God into a black hole whose all consuming causation sucks all other space into itself. "Sovereignty" seems to be a way of saying that all space belongs to God, rather than, as the Easter Vigil has it, "All time belongs to Him." Divine sovereignty seems then to be a way of saying human enslavement. It's hard to blame secular folks for thinking so, when the tribe of priests seem to think that freedom meant no more than clerical exercise of coercion on God's behalf.

Since the nineteenth century writers have envisaged politics as the management of social space, and of freedom as operating in space, as the preservation of self-sovereignty. They allocated to Christian institutions specialized areas in which the sacred remained sovereign, and soon after the administrators of space made room for every cult, so long as the Cult agreed to remain within its own territory. This management of the Cults by the State was organized so as to keep out the space invaders, the theocrats. And so secularization seems to relate to space and the government of it.

The secular*ist* conceives of the clerical and the secular powers as being in contestation for space, and for a limited quantity of it. So what had been a distinction becomes an unequivocal divide. A battle must be waged for *Lebensraum*. God is conceived by the secularist as greedily consuming *all of the space*, and so the concept of God becomes antithetical to humanity. The secularized State wants to make an end to history, in that it wills to prevent the human impulse to rise above time and give meaning to it. The secularized State does not admit eternal truths. The secularized State ensures that a multitude of religious claims makes monolatry the fierce and obstinate exception to the rule. This is what happened in Roman Imperial times.

The Roman Imperium claimed to be spreading *romanitas*, not secularization, and the Americans of the twentieth century wanted to extend the benefits of the American way of life to everyone. It seems to be a bit of a stretch to call the polytheistic culture of the Roman Empire *secularist*. The question, though, is whether in Roman imperial times, the polytheism was not a bit of a pretense, integral to the "bread and circuses" which kept the show on the road.

Empire builders know how to make space sacred. Once the Roman Republic had died in civil war, and empire had become a thing, it quickly became a sacred thing. The victor in that civil war, and first emperor of Rome, Augustus Caesar, was offered the funeral rites of one who had been elevated to deity at the moment of death. Augustus's apotheosis meant that his successor, Tiberius Caesar was designated "son of god." Doubtless the "deity" of the emperors was known to be a political fiction, and inspired little genuine *pietas*. The Emperor Vespian informed his courtiers that he was dying by observing "O dear I think I am becoming a god." The fiction of the emperor's divinity registered the experienced sacrality of the empire itself. Rome pretended to believe in the divine personae of the emperors because it really and truly believed in the sacrality of its Imperium, its right to extend its laws, roads, and dominion over the known world.

Rome came out of the civil war as an empire, not a republic, because only an emperor could govern the vast, multicultural empire Rome had become. Generals, and their armies, proved too vital to a subject empire to be subordinate to a senate. Once you make your space the ultimate purpose of purposes, you make it sacred. The same spatial thinking which gives us secularization gives us sacred geographies, particularly empires. It's when empires become elephantine that they become "sacred."

The Rome Empire was a theocracy in being literally—if fictionally—being ruled by a god: it took the fiction of the emperor's divinity rather literally. We tend to associate theocracy with fanatical devotion to one religion alone. It seems to suggest belief in one deity, whose worship is uniformly imposed upon all subjects of the theocracy. But most empires have been benignly multi-religious, with the imperialists encouraging the retention of local cults in the lands they colonized. British imperialists were annoyed by those Christians missionaries in India who irritated the natives by proposing that theirs was the only true faith. Empires do not encourage the restless heart. In this, too, the Roman Empire followed the law of the Elephants.

The Roman Empire authorized and proscribed religious cults. It laid down the law for sacred as well as secular institutions. Ancient Rome was thus a multi-religious theocracy, legalizing all cults which were willing in principle to include the person of the emperor in their cult. It let the Jews go their own way, and dispense with emperor worship, because Jewish monolatry was too stubborn to bring to heel. Statolatry is a pragmatic theocracy. Statolatry? Well yes, because the God the Romans revered was not the person of the emperor but the State and its reasons. They allowed him his pretense of divinity in order to put a human mask on the real locus of omnicompetence. The public space was filled, and filled entirely, with the person of the emperor, representative of the State. The person of the emperor was the human mask on the Roman State, which erected many fine laws, but whose fundamental element was raw power.

Ancient, elephantine Rome was broken by the obstinacy of the Christians, with their narrow, dogmatic insistence upon worship of Father, Son, and Holy Spirit. The early Christians preached that the ancient, original, accept no substitutes Sky-Father was none too happy about the centuries of his neglect and the cheerful descent of human worship into a supermarket of religions, each loudly selling its wares, barking out bargain-basement promises of enlightenment through initiation. It was evident to someone with omniscient eyes to see that in their quest for someone worthy of their deepest desire, human persons had worshiped a series of masks, behind which was evanescent smoke and mirrors. Knowing that polytheism and polylatry, the worship of many gods, were the consequence of blindly searching for the One God, the Sky-Father entered upon a paradoxical project. To remind the peoples that there is but one God, the Sky-Father showed them his face and hands, and let them hear his voice in the tongue of his Word. "But when the fulness of the time was come, God sent forth his Son" (Galatians 4:4): the fullness of time was the moment when history arrived at its meaning. Christianity was the resurgence of the primitive and aboriginal monotheism, renewed through touching and seeing the face of the one God.

The Romans of the third and fourth centuries regarded this new religious cult, not as a renaissance of monotheism but as a new propagation of atheism—because the Christians would not play at being polytheistic and would not venerate the emperor. The Christians who broke the back of the Roman Empire had no public space to call their own. The belief that time was on their side liberated them to challenge those who had power of life and death over them. Human temporality or secularity itself was the means by which Death had been broken. Time could be harnessed to eternity in the space of the human body: this belief was their manumission.

Quintus Aurelius Symmachus (345–402) knew of the Christian claim, and he could not give his assent to it. Symmachus illustrates the Roman, imperial way of resolving the competing claims of religions. In conscious objection to the narrow "bigotry" of Christians, Symmachus complained that "we gaze up at the same stars; the sky covers us all; the same universe encompasses us. Does it matter what practical system we adopt in our search for the Truth? The heart of so great a mystery cannot be reached by following one road only."[1]

The Romans threaded their empire with straight roads, up and down which they executed rapid troop movements. The Roman roads were the real symbol of Imperium in operation. The roads made the armies of Rome inescapable and indominatable. The roads left the subject peoples with no place to hide. The roads were the means of enslavement.

As a Roman, Symmachus knew that roads are just about power, that road building assists the imposition of Roman rule by force, and that straight roads make possible the retention of power. If roads are all about power, there must be "many roads" to God: that is, many little coteries, cults, and clubs pretending to guard access to the divine. So then the question is "who guards the guards," *Quis custodiet ipsos custodes? As a believer in romanitas*, Symmachus saw through particular cultic claims, and came to believe that such particularist claims are all about power. Symmachus grasped that every cult of a particular god is simply seeking to put one over its adherents: the elite of priests secretly know better. So Symmachus tried to bypass them, and achieve the perfect, Archimedean leverage in which he saw through them all. Symmachus taught that it ought to be an indifferent matter by which Road we reach the ultimate. Because the Roads are not to be trusted, not one of them: all of them lead to Rome.

---

[1] Quintus Aurelius Symmachus, quoted in Joseph Ratzinger, *Truth and Tolerance: Christian Belief and World Religions*, translated by Henry Taylor, (San Francisco, CA: Ignatius, 2004), p. 176.

Symmachus preached an agnosticism of the sovereign spark. This agnosticism which Symmachus advocated presumes that religions are just about power, and that we should reserve sovereignty to ourselves by not choosing between them and giving our assent to one set of priests. Symmachus's "many roads to God" is no challenge to the Roman Empire. The agnosticism of the sovereign spark accepts the basic Roman dictate that power has the last word. If power has the last word, then we are all slaves, our countries, our property, and our bodies, right down the bone, belonging to some higher power. If power is the last word, freedom is the ownership on a disembodied spark which one identifies as one's own "soul." The sovereign spark maintains that freedom is the curation of a disembodied spark, floating in the Universe with no direction home, and no space to make its home.

A very different, and superficially less admirable Roman, Flavius Valerius Aurelius Constantinus Augustus, chose a different kind of freedom. Emperor Constantine chose to give away his power over the religious cults. He gave away the pretense to deity. When in the year 310 Emperor Constantine legalized the Christian religion he liberated the pockets of real human secularity within the empire. The pinch of incense had become optional, and thus the State had ceased to insist upon its own divinity, ceased to be "theocratic" and chose to occupy secular space. Constantine conceded that the empire exists in secular, and not in sacred time: when he legendarily marked his soldiers' shields with the sign of the Cross he admitted that it is God who shapes historical time. Western Church–State relations began in a tacit act of self-secularization on the part of the State. Constantine stepped back and permitted the worship of something incommensurably greater than the Roman Empire.

All he had done was to recognize Christianity as one of many legal religions. The Church lives in an era of "secularity" when it is recognized by the State as one amongst many legally permissible "cults" or religious institutions. The era of "secularity" which Constantine inaugurated was one in which the Church was permitted to put her claims alongside other claimants. In this short-lived era of secularity, between Constantine and Theodosius, who closed the pagan temples, Christianity thrived. Its intelligent defenders thrilled to participate in a war of words with other cults. The Apologists took up the mantle of the martyrs in sowing the seeds of the Church in human hearts. They used the force of human and divine words against the pagan philosophers.

The last of the great Apologists was Augustine, challenging the pagans to produce evidence of a more lasting source of happiness than membership in the eternal "City of God." The apologists did not experience this "secular" era as one of "de-sacralization," but as an opportunity for conversion and baptism of pagan souls. Augustine's great book, *The City of God* belittles the glamour of the empires as mere inflated egotism. It does not belittle the secular: the secular is not the city of man, opposed to the City of God. The secular is the battleground, where the two cities meet and fight. The secular is the historical.

A merely *secular* state encourages a plurality of religions, each staking its claim to be true. On the other hand, a *secularized*, theocratic state does not give a religion freedom to say it is true. The precondition of the authorization of a cult by the multi-religious empire is that it makes no claim to exclusive truth and is not too red-neck, savage or downright unsophisticated to acknowledge that all gods are relative. Relative to what? To the "Ultimate" behind the curtain—a curtain drawn up by the imperialists, and behind which we may never peek for a moment, lest we find a silly old Wizard of Oz. The empty throne of the global religious "Ultimate," the "Ultimate" beyond all the many gods beyond the gods worshiped by historical human beings, is thought to be one of the dirty secrets of Imperialism.

Freely rising above time and shaping it is part of what makes us human, and different from most of the other animals. What about space? If space is of no moment, we may as well be sovereign sparks, floating in a homeless universe. Are we so sure that all the other animals divide up space and create little territories for themselves, but human beings can do well enough without it?

Let's go back to those roads, those spatial emblems of Imperium, created by Roman soldiers with pick axes, shovels, and rocks. I've walked on the road created by the Seventh legion across the flat plains of the Meseta in central Spain. Its pebbles have smacked on my feet as they have done to the soles of thousands of travelers and pilgrims over 2,000 years. The roads were built in the service of Roman power. But isn't walking along a road, rather than cross country or through a forest something human beings like to do? Don't we humanize a region when we build tracks across it for others to share? We do not just make tracks, as the bears and the wolves and bison do; we build roads for others to walk upon. Sacralizing space is something we share with the animals, if sacralizing space, includes without being reducible to, walling off a territory. But that doesn't make it any less humane, or any less of a communication of ourselves to others. It's initially about power, but the network of roads, like leylines, carries its own magical power of humanization. Over the centuries, groups of people, and not just armies, make their way along them. Traveling a road is also a metaphor for seeking the one God. Traveling a road is an exercise of freedom.

Sacralizing space has more of an animal smell to it than discovering the value of time; that's often quite literally the tang of urine and of sweat. We mark our territory with our human smells. And let the fragrance rise, like an evening sacrifice. No matter how far it puts us on all fours with the quadrupeds, we venerate our gods in and through our sacralizing of spaces, the construction of cumuli, temples, stupa, high places, pilgrimage sites, the residences of sacred bones and other precious objects, and Cathedrals.

Our sacralization of space is a metaphorical enactment of our experience of conscience, as an inner moral compass by which we navigate the ethical cosmos. The right way is *Tao* for Confucians, and for Jews it is "the halakha," the way to walk. Truth and meaning may be in time, but the good inhabits space, and its enactment occurs upon a circumscribed stage. Of course space is "only" a metaphor for moral agency. But it's a "real metaphor": we speak of falling into crime, not rising into it, for reasons which have to do with our embodiment. We speak of upright citizens because of insights imposed upon us by the shape of the human body. Taking a fall from any kind of height is damaging.

It's said that people who become habituated to navigating in their cars using a GPS lose their sense of direction. They become reliant on the GPS and do not build up an internal visual map of the region they drive around. It's in the same way, metaphorically, that the Ultimate, beyond all the religions, supplants the exercise of conscience, of moral reasoning. The GPS is guiding the driver from outside and "above" his or her situation. The Ultimate, outside and above the halakha and the Tao of any given, historical religion, makes its decisions with its bird's-eye view of our moral task and vocation. It takes the place of the generation and inhabitation of a moral, visual map of our life situations, and of our exercise of freedom in the means and ways, the avenues, through which we approach the Good. It's impossible freely to enact a moral code from outside and above all moral codes. If one tries to chart the roads from outside and above all the codes, all one can do is passively obey the GPS as it mispronounces all the local place names. All localities are equally alien and foreign to it, because it inhabits none. The external GPS replaces our own conscience.

And this is the deeper reason why Symmachus has nothing authentically counter-cultural to say as a citizen of a theocracy whose

"Ultimate" is the hidden hand of the State itself. His "Ultimate," reached by no particular road, enslaves all of its pilgrims. The trackless path to the Ultimate is not just the path of sovereign sparks, who have decided not to take their orders from the Priests of any one particular Cult. It is the path of slavers, and their slaves.

Human beings have tried to uncover the track back to their first, prehistorical monotheism along various different roads. The Romans tried to find the "One" which would unify an empire in the State. They said, in effect, behind their hands, the State is the One. Three centuries after the fall of the Western Roman Empire, a new monotheism arose in the deserts of Arabia. Instead of making a god of the State, it made a state out of God. This new religion presented God as constituted by a unity of imperial absoluteness. God was found to have a state-like unity of decree and of purpose; the unity of a call to submission. The purpose of this unadulterated unity was to unify mankind in one single people; the command of this deity was complete submission to the Will of the One. This God had no use for the freedom of human kinds; they were not to co-create their destinies but to submit to them. Human beings were not to cooperate with this God or with the decadent polytheisms they observed outside the religion of submission. Those who submit themselves to this one God could not say with Lacordaire, "The rights of God are the rights of humanity." The Muslims were sacrificed on the altar of the secularizing theocracy of the Martian Robots.

14

The Bodhissatva Henri-Dominique Lacordaire

Cult was the first of the two to protest his cause, demanding to speak to the Robot in charge when his captors sent him below deck, clapped in irons. "No Robots on this ship," came the jeering reply, sending the bumptious man into near despair. The pirates dragged him below deck, still weeping, and mockingly thrust him into the hollow shell of a discarded robotic propulsion unit. Dejected and dehydrated, he was forced to stand in the armored accoutrements of the Tin Man while his angelic tormentors frolicked and skipped around him singing "We are off to see the Wizard, the wonderful wizard of Oz."

Pistis too was soon stowed in the lower quarters of the pirate ship, its bearings fixed for Mars. She was on her way to the auction block. The plunge from exaltation to debasement had been so sudden as to knock most of the heart out of this free spirit. Reports of the Sky-Father, the upstart gods, and the fallen angels drifted about the galaxies in strange, distorting Chinese whispers. But legend had never reached Oz of the deal between the Robots from Mars and their erstwhile Masters. She could only wonder whether the *National Inquirer* had it right all along? Do aliens travel the skies in UFO's abducting human beings? It was clear that her kidnapping and current shackling could not be the doing of the Robots, since her jailors made no pretense of liberating her. She knew of course that our Earth's Overlords had conquered dozens of planets, claiming to set them on the conveyor belt to happiness. She guessed now that some of the Martians' subjects fell through the cracks, refusing to be relieved of their tragic propensities for egotism and violence. The crew who handled her roughly into the lower quarters had not seemed like ruffians or outcasts, but like decadent aristocracy who had fallen on hard times.

"They *arrre* completely self-centered," said a Voice, one who remembered the post-Revolutionary dregs of the aristocrats of the *ancien régime*. "Insane with self-absorption. Drugged to the eyeballs with delusions." Pistis struggled to see in the pitch dark room, but couldn't make out a figure. "Did they get you as well?" she asked. "From France?" The invisible friar's accent gave him away. "*C'est vrrrai, je suis Francaise*," the Voice answered, "and I'm a free man. Not a prisoner on this ship." "Are you one of them?" Pistis inquired fearlessly. The Voice was beginning to materialize and as he did, she could make out in the lightless room the outlines of a white cassock, white socks, black tennis shoes, and a black cape. "I am," the Dominican replied grandly 'Ze Bodhissatva "Enri Dominique Lacordairrrrrre." His face was exactly like her statue in the apartment, so Pistis had to believe him. "I've been enslaved," explained Pistis. "With my friends … " "You are not a slave," said the Friar.

"Are you here to rescue me? And Gnosis?" Pistis asked confidently. "*Mais non*," the Friar replied with gloomy satisfaction. "You are 'ere to rescue humanité." Pistis didn't weep, much. It was what she had wanted to do since the flattenings and the elephants, the genocide of the non-compliant Muslims, and the reduction of humanity to bit parts in the automated factory that fallen Earth had become. "This ship is bound for Mars. You must find Prometheus and unchain him." Now Pistis protested. "Isn't that a job for Gnosis?" He was the one who still thinks science has the answer to everything! After all that's happened to us, after the Robots! The girl added rebelliously, "The last thing we need back home is more technology." Didn't the nineteenth-century Dominican know that humanity might soon shuffle off its skin and finding nothing but a robot underneath! "The ghost in the machine," answered the Frenchman vaguely. "The machines back home will be lucky to have ghosts in them pretty soon," said Pistis furiously. "That's what I want to save us from, from out of control science. We don't need one more Dr. Frankenstein! Send Gnosis if you want to unchain Prometheus! If he hadn't been there none of this would have happened," she concluded irrationally. Pistis was spitting with indignation at the ridiculous vocation imposed upon her by her patron saint. "Yes and we should have burnt Galileo too," teased 'Enri-Dominique, with an infuriating Gallic shrug.

Now the saintly defender of human freedom against its secularist and its clerical opponents pulled himself up. The master of rhetoric was not going to give one of his fabled sermons. They did not have four hours. The pirate ship was rushing toward Mars at light speed. "*You* are going to unchain Prometheus because *you* have faith! Unbind Invention and give him the gift of faith. Let's see what he will do then." The Friar made the Sign over the girl, and then rapidly melted from sight. "What about Gnosis?" asked the girl urgently. She caught a fleeting whisper about another wing. Tugging her head upward on her chain, she watched through the Perspex port-hole as the patron saint of liberty returned into unending light. "Go ahead! Just beam up and leave me here!" said Pistis sarcastically to the receding figure. "Don't even bother to untie me!" But Lacordaire was gone and there was a faint, urgent tapping at the door.

The friar paid a second visit that evening, to console and strengthen a priest who had long since forgotten his vocation. Cult had the instinct to worship, but had never had a clue how to exercise it. A born fan-boy since long before the Robots erected their altars to the Unknown God, Cult had spent his life in a fervor of misdirected worship. Now for two brief minutes, Lacordaire gave the thwarted acolyte a vision of adoration. He showed him Paradise. Not the semi-satirical Paradise imagined by Euripides, but the real deal. Cult saw the Throne and the Lamb upon it. Seemingly thousands of miles back from the Throne, he saw the Saints of all the ages, rocking the heavens with a rhythmic and raucous love song. Right there in front of the

Throne were the Newcomers who did not yet know the ropes well enough to take a stand at the back. They had been judged and found worthy by the One God and now they schooled Cult in worship. Face-flat on their prayer mats, the army of Sufis, Shi'a, and Sunnis prostrated themselves and then raised their hands, bowed, and rose, over and again rising and falling from their knees in an ecstatic dance of carefree and gracious love. They heard the eternal Duet keeping eternal time by drums and cymbals, and they rose and fell in time with the drums and the clashing of the symbols, chanting their "Fiat," "Fiat," as the drum beat in each heart and the Voices rang in their ears. Each swung to his own unique drummer; each swayed to the one Spirit, Creator of creativity. Cult, who had once been enraptured by the Robotic cry of "I, I", heard now the human and divine voices singing in rounds, "Thy will be done." No longer slaves, the saints were worshiping in time to the wild, throaty chorusing of the old-timers. For a second, Cult burned with shame at the sight of the men whose martyrdom had once left him untouched. In that instant of contrition he was emancipated from the last taint of his idolatry. Like the newly minted saints, he became a free man, a worshiper, a lover.

Pistis had no such vision to warm her as she listened to the squeak and rattle at her door. How do you know who is scratching on the other side of the door? It takes a bit of faith and hope, as you wait in the dark, and the clock ticks, ticks, and the ship begins to whoosh an unmistakable descent. Pistis could do nothing but sit and listen to the rasp of metal on metal. Was it her rescuer patiently cutting through the lock on the cabin door? She believed it to be so, and that kept her from crying out in fear and anguish as she sat for hours listening to the methodical sawing. At the last moment, just as she was holding at bay the thought that the rasp was her jailers mockingly shaking their keys, Gnosis popped his nerdy head into the cabin, his biros still clipped into his shirt-pocket. The two were tight lipped, both too wary of alerting a guard to say much. "It's pretty ramshackle for a

Robot ship," Gnosis whispered cheerfully in her ear, as he set to work on her leash. "Picked up the file up in the boiler room," he added sotto voce, rather proud of his uncharacteristic display of manual dexterity. "So you weren't in the other wing?" she hissed. "What? What wing! It's a spaceship, not a giant bird!" "We are headed to Mars," she said. "How do you know that?" Gnosis demanded. "I overheard someone say so," answered Pistis wisely. The scientist raced through his filing now, the task urgent, as the pirate ship descended toward its dock. They seemed to be circling, held in a queue, while they awaited a docking gate. The momentary delay gave Gnosis just the time he needed to finish sawing Pistis's heavy chain, and to cut that fetter from the wall. At the moment when the ship bumped noisily to the ground, he raised the chain above his head and thrashed the port-hole. He had broken it! Pistis climbed over his shoulders, through the hole. Tying the chain to the port-hook, she lowered it to the man, who eagerly made his own ascent. Greeted by a rabbit's warren of squishy pipes, they fled headlong into the first open sewer they met, and were down the hatch before the Pirate Captain opened the cabin door.

"We need to stay close to the dock," gasped Gnosis breathlessly after they had long lost sight of the port, and were lost in a spaghetti-maze of rubbery pipes. "We are here for a reason," Pistis began, lamely. "Not the God lecture. Not now," said Gnosis firmly. "We need to find Prometheus," Pistis went on, gathering courage. "What the hell would he be doing on Mars? If this is Mars, which we only have your word for. Or what you overheard," Gnosis concluded diplomatically. He truly hoped that he was not on an unknown planet with a woman of artistic temperament who had been driven insane by her ordeal and was now determined to initiate a search for a nonexistent figure of Greek mythology. The pipes seemed to spiral on endlessly underground, in umpteen curleques, as if they were inside the small intestines of a bull. "You'd expect to find *Mars*, if we are where you say we are. Not Prometheus!" "Roman god of war. Not the Greek god who gave fire." It was a fairly weak start, certainly, but this was in the first time Gnosis had made a joke since the Martian conquest of Earth, and he had some catching up to do. He was doing his best to humor the girl. She needed to keep up her spirits until they could stow away on an earth-bound ship and get out of this inferno, with its horrible smell of drying blood. Where one wormy pipe ended, half a dozen more stringy open mouths were laid out. "I didn't expect Mars to be like the inside of a stomach," Gnosis said grimly. Pistis answered, "It smells like a butcher's shop. Like offal." Gnosis wondered if he *should* humor Pistis's insanity. Maybe he should order her to snap out of it. "What would the god who gave us the power to make tools be doing on a shite dead planet like Mars? The climate is terrible! Its hot!" "It's fiery," Pistis agreed politely, adding, "What are these huge feathers?" "Probably came here from one of the cargo ships," said Gnosis carelessly. "Maybe they used them to bargain with the natives. Like Wampum beads," he added. As they wandered toward the end of one pipe, the two human beings began to hear sounds like cawing and rustling. The ground was pocked with chalky white patches. "Bird shit" said Pistis impolitely. "Don't leap to conclusions," snapped Gnosis. "Don't guess! Do you even know what a hypothesis is ?" Then they heard inhuman screams.

15

The New Prometheus

Turning through the umpteenth S bend, and finding themselves at the end of the slithery pipe, the pair had no choice but reluctantly to exit their intestinal trench-line. The screams went to eleven now, and they could see eagles, fighting in the sky over bits of raw and bloody meat. In the distance, silhouetted against a mountain range which pygmied the Himalayas, stood an enormous man. Taller than the Statue of Liberty and out-Elephanting all of the Robots' Plexiglas pachyderms, the Fire-Bringer was nailed by his ankles and wrists to the rock. They had to shout to make themselves heard above the cacophony of eagles squawking and over the bellowing of a Greek god.

High away in the distance they could see eagles fighting to the death over the abundance of bloody liver and guts which sprouted from Prometheus' belly. The tiny pair of human animals knew that those greedy and selfish birds would gulp them down as an appetizer. Not wanting to become the object of avian sarcasm about the tastelessness of mortal flesh, they hid themselves as best they could behind Prometheus' odiferous, bunioned feet.

"It's a dream come true," yelled Gnosis, gesturing at the grisly scene. He shouted "how did you *know*?" "I didn't *know*," Pistis howled meekly in reply. "KNOW-HOW, KNOW-HOW, KNOW-HOW" replied the echo. Pistis waited out the echo and added, "a Voice spoke and I had faith in what I heard." FAITH HEARING, FAITH HEARING echoed around the endless range of sheer rock. It's very difficult not to get angry when you are shouting. "Don't give me that nonsense," Gnosis bellowed. "Mars is peopled by Supermen, and you better believe it if you want to get out alive." SUPERMEN! SUPERMEN ALIVE! SUPERMEN GET OUT OF ALIVE echoed around the chalky cliff faces. "He's out of reach," bawled Pistis, looking around desperately. DOVER BEACH! boomed the echo helpfully.

Pistis rubbed her hand against the vertiginous mountain-side. "Its chalk," she said. She wondered at how the eagles seeing the superfluity of food could murder and die for scraps and morsels of the gods' ever-growing flesh. "Terrible vibes," she screamed at Gnosis, Looking away from the greedy scenes above, she saw that the ground was spewn, not only with decaying offal, but with feathers, bits of beak and claw, and, here and there, buffalo-size bones, thighs and wings, pecked bare and whitening, like the unburied remains of an aerial battle. She seized a bare thigh and walking over to Prometheus' right ankle began to hack at the rock in which Prometheus' right ankle was pinioned. Gnosis took a sharp claw and began to scratch alongside her. As Pistis had guessed, the chalk was soft, and after several hours of hollowing the rock containing the metal, as darkness fell they triumphantly began to slide a single nail out of the cliffside. With night falling thickly, then, Pistis pulled on the inside of the Promethean ankle and Gnose on the outer side, and they yanked out a nail like a pole vault.

Meantime, the sounds of the aerial combat had quietened. These eagles had only to think it was night to return to their nests and tuck in until dawn and the regrowth of the god's vitals. The pair were nearly crushed to death when, feeling one ankle free, Prometheus lifted it and began vigorously to scratch it against his left leg. The god peered down at the tiny creatures and had the good sense to whisper, "Good evening, Mr. Know-How! Enchanted to meet you Miss Faith Ears! Come up here where I can get a better look at you! Don't be shy! Climb up my leg! Plenty of hair on there still!" So clasping the thick strands of divine hair, the two used his follicles as a system of belays to scale his bandy legs. Just above belly height, and saving them from the horrors of bleeding entrails, his luxurious beard afforded them spindly leverage to his throat and shoulders. "What a beard," said Pistis politely. "Bastards are always pulling bits out to make their nests," said the god, modestly deflecting her compliment.

The deposition of the god was fraught with terrors. The long vertical climb had knocked the strength out of the pair, and the approach of Sunday morning was signaled by ominous sounds of rustling and sleepy, unmelodious cawings. They were exposed, and vulnerable, though in later days Gnosis would mimic Pistis cheerfully insisting, "the beard is all the camouflage we need!" Both of them knew that their limbs would be ripped, fought over, and gobbled by half a dozen eagles if they attempted to get to the nail which pinioned Prometheus' right hand. Freezing cold, covered in sweat, and cowering under the god's chin, they heard a sound like an old lawnmower, chuntering, coughing, constant attempts to restart, with many back-fires, and sudden bursts of energy. Neither of them had given a thought to Cult since Friday night. Now they saw the pious bartender, enclosed in a tin propulsion unit, desperately attempting to gain enough steam to rise above his pursuers. Cult was bobbling on the ground and taking small hops and leaps like a cricket, while the propulsion suit blew out steams of hot air behind him. All that was visible of him was his feet and arms, sticking out of the roaring tube. Every time he hit the ground one of the pirates would attempt to grab his foot, and every time Cult's suit took a vertical leap, he lost them. Gnosis really did say, and Pistis swore to it, "A propulsion unit! It's a sort of reverse vacuum cleaner. I wanted to design one." "Shut up," said Pistis, "and do something to help Cult!" If the pirates, hot in pursuit of the flying treasure, espied the two, their adventure would end in chains. "Push the levers down," hissed Gnosis. Desperation gave Cult a momentary burst of imagination, and he pulled the levers toward himself, causing his stallion to rocket upward and land in the follicular shrubbery encasing the deity's throat.

The propulsion machine was still buzzing, and Gnosis and Pistis desperately disentangled him from the luxuriant beard. Pistis seized his right arm, and Gnosis clung to his left. The eagles backed off warily from the roaring rocket, giving the trio free reign to hop frantically along the deity's right arm. Expertly steered toward the nails by Gnosis on the left and Pistis on the right, the tube crashed into the cliff-face ten feet above their target, denting the soft rock and causing an avalanche of chalk and pebbles to bounce down the mountain. When the dust cleared, they saw Prometheus vigorously completing their work, ripping his hand out of the wall. With his right hand freed, he tore out the nail which had held his left hand. "You are no longer in thrall to Zeus," said Cult, firmly, "Receive the breath of the Holy Spirit." Pistis was momentarily put-out: the hope of performing a lay baptism of Prometheus had kept her going through the long night. He had the rubric completely wrong, anyway. "Those are not the words of baptism," she said impolitely. "It doesn't matter," said Prometheus kindly, "we have to let the clergy get on with it, whatever mess they make of the liturgy. Cult is right. My punishment is over, and Cult has given me the grace to redeem myself, by rescuing the Earth."

The four knew that Prometheus had not been released from captivity out of cosmic mercy alone. Rather, the lover of human beings had been released for a providential task: to liberate the Earth from its thralldom. How was Prometheus to defeat the Robots single-handed? Gnosis was silent. He could not look the hirsute giant in the eye. It was too embarrassing to make conversation with a Greek deity. Finally he mumbled, stupidly, "Zeus is pissing through a sieve."[1] In his desperate attempt to think of something to say to the god, Gnosis had quoted a line which stayed with him from his humorless Comedy course—Aristophanes' mocking the anthropomorphic fables with a blasphemous description of a Mediterranean downpour. So nesting

---

[1] Aristophanes, *The Clouds*, translated by William Arrowsmith (New York: Meridean, 1994).

the rocket in his beard, with Gnosis and Pistis clinging to the priest's arms, Prometheus leapt toward the earth. And, standing astride the moon, he began relentlessly to piss on the Robot ships as they circumnavigated our Earth. He pissed on the ships, and the god's urine created a monsoon, flooding the earth with more water than it had seen since Noah and the Paleolithic melting of the ice-caps. The supermassive elephants were drenched and began themselves to spout rivers of liquid from their trunks. In the cities, and in the hillside towns, outside every home, candles were being dampened, drowned, and finally quenched by streams of living waters. Prometheus pissed on, marking out the territory that belongs to the Logos, the Word, and Reason of God. He aimed his transcendent arc of fiery, masculine urine at what belongs to God and equally belongs to man.[2] He reawakened consciences and moral sensors which were dead in the ground, buried in the desiccated soil of human hearts. He pissed on the celebrities in their obedience collars, electrocuting most of them. He inundated the self-designated Holy Land and the Robot cities alike, nailing the human habitat with his marking. Prometheus slashed secularity back onto the globe, healthy soil into which the sacred could be planted. The newly converted Prometheus re-baptized the Robots' Oz, and remade it as our dear Earth.

The Robots were confused and then enraged by the sudden extinguishing of their food source. They began, then, systematically to destroy one another. Starved of the fruits of worship, the Robots turned on one another, seeking the only good which they knew, that of domination. The beneficiaries of the erstwhile Theocracy watched as war in heaven filled the skies for thirteen minutes of human time. The cacophony of a thousand dog-fights rattled in their ear drums, as the rotating Eyes fought their civil war. Pandemonium

---

[2] For the "arc of transcendence," see Camille Paglia, *Sexual Personae: Art and Decadence from Nefertiti to Emily Dickinson* (New Haven, CT: Yale University Press, 2001), pp. 21 ff.

reigned in the heavens, even as the Theocracy descended into the pure violence at its core.

Little boys rushed about the streets collecting bits of useless weaponry, turning it upon their fellows in mock battles that raged in the streets from Vladivostok to Guadalajara. What had begun as school boy waterfights during the Promethean flood turned into joyous war-games, as the human young began to have fun for the first time they could remember. Discarding every tenet of safety, every fear for life and limb, they played and they fought for treasure as the battle played out in the skies above. Boyish laughter rang out around the globe. The sun began to peek through the satellite network. And then it was over as suddenly and as sweepingly as it had begun. The Martian fleet had once again been consumed by mutual self-destruction. Prometheus had turned their one single will to conquest against itself. A few limping Robot star-ships slipped away, no doubt to recuperate and exercise their misanthropic mission elsewhere, on a less ungrateful planet. When they arrived home on Mars, the surviving Robot crew really did say to the Eagle-Angels, "you had just one job to do."

The earth had been saved by a baptized and Christianized Prometheus, with no little help from the French Bodhissatva and three human persons, Pistis 475, Gnostic 777, and Theodore Cult. Pretty soon it seemed that most of humanity who had survived the flood had secretly been in the resistance. They were, it was true, exhausted with having to live up to Robotic rather than human standards of behavior. They were glad to be human again instead of being BOTTs, and glad that the earth was once again our "earth," and not Oz. They took their baptism in the fiery piss of Prometheus seriously. Most of the global South were relieved that the defeat of the Robots did not mean the return to an agrarian, subsistence economy. Mongolians, Chinese, Siberians, Serbs, and even Argentinians and Brazilians were glad when everyone went back to their normal human names. The Catholics who had migrated to the Holy Land, calling themselves the

"Holy Church," were excited for the prospect of a new conclave. The unholy Catholics hoped for the election of a jolly overweight pope who would regularize their situation. The Wee Freeby Catholics came up from Underground, bringing with them the half-dozen Jewish families who had survived the Robots' resettling of the Holy Land. No one on earth was sufficiently pessimistic to do anything but rejoice at the dismantling of the Sleeping Room and the Recycling Machine. Most people had come to see that the world's troubles were not best solved by eradicating troubled people. They had come to see that they had *chosen* to be Robots, whilst all along *desiring* to be Prometheus. They had learned that when humanity chooses and elects to be governed from the most perfect point outside of humanity, all that results is the alienation of humanity from its own deepest desires.

Billions of people tuned in to watch the quiet ceremony at the Vatican at which Faith was wedded to Reason. Millions of women shed tears when the couple exchanged their vows. Some TV scientists wept with chagrin but not so many. The Catholics would have preferred it if the saintly Cardinal Pistisino had presided but the couple had insisted on Theo Cult, so he did his bumbling best with the sound of heavenly trumpets forever in his ears and thousands of Web Cams trained upon him. Cardinal Pistisino was soon elected Pope, creating a job vacancy for those temperamentally inclined to sedevacantism. His first act was belatedly to canonize Henri-Dominique Lacordaire. Lacordaire's canonization was celebrated with a gigantic display of firecrackers: bonfires were lit from London to Beijing, and the ruins of the Martian ships were burned to a crisp. Folks from East to West were glad that the defeat of the Robots at the hands of Prometheus meant that science was put to use in the service of humanity. They rubbed their eyes and remembered the meaning of philanthropy. Instead of serving science and scientists, science became a gift which helped people create a humane culture. Once Prometheus dedicated himself to cooperating with the One God who turns his face to us in his Word, he put all of his techniques, once more, at the service of the human good. Scientific rationality would not—for some time—enslave the human world, but help to lead it toward its destiny, of free cooperation with the one true God. The gift that baptized Prometheus gave the human race which he loved was not a new technology like fire, but simply humanity itself. The gift was humanity on fire with human creativity, love of knowledge, and freedom. In coming to themselves, human beings awoke to recall that they wanted to transition into gods, children of the one Father, and not into robots.

Envoi

There could thus be—let us dare this paradox—a Christian Prometheus ... May [humanity] pursue, as long as this world lasts, the activities of Prometheus: let him light a new fire in each century, the material basis for new human strides—... But, at the same time, let him beg for the descent of the only Fire without whose burning nothing can be purified, consumed, saved, eternalized: *Emitte Spiritum tuum et creabuntur, et renovabis faciem terrae— Send forth your Spirit and they will be created, and you will renew the face of the earth.*[1]

Prometheus initiates the freedom and advance of man, and then begins to suffer ... The more part of the religious imagination leads an autonomous life in the secular world, the more it must lead the life of prayer. The more it discovers the outside world, the more it must lead its own inward life. The more it does not any longer impose its own symbols or referential meanings on the world, the more it must be in touch with its own history and forms. The more it gives up Christ, the more it must find him. ... For, finally, the autonomy of the secular, the autonomy of the world, comes from the outside we call God. It is a creation of the outside, and in that sense a creation of the secular by the sacred. ... Autonomy is not a defiance but a grace.[2]

---

[1] Henri de Lubac, *The Drama of Atheist Humanism*, translated by Edith M. Riley, Ann Englund Nash, and Mark Sebanc (San Francisco, CA: Ignatius, 1995), pp. 420 and 468.

[2] William Lynch, *Christ and Prometheus: A New Image of the Secular* (Notre Dame, IN: Notre Dame University Press, 1970), pp. 59 and 139–140.

Bibliography

Aquinas, Thomas, *Summa Theologiae*, trans. Fathers of the English Dominican Province (Westminster, MD: Christian Classics, 1981).

Aristophanes, *The Clouds*, trans. William Arrowsmith (Meridian: New York, 1994).

Batuman, Elif, "The World's Oldest Temple and the Dawn of Civilization," *New Yorker* (December 19 and 26, 2011).

De Lubac, Henri, *The Drama of Atheist Humanism*, trans. Edith M. Riley, AnnEnglund Nash, and Mark Sebanc (San Francisco, CA: Ignatius, 1995).

De Lubac, Henri, *The Discovery of God*, trans. Alexander Dru (Grand Rapids, MI: Eerdmans, 1996).

Gregory XVI, *Mirari Vos* (1832).

Lynch, William F., *Christ and Prometheus: A New Image of the Secular* (Notre Dame, IN: Notre Dame University Press, 1970).

Nietzsche, Friedrich, *Beyond Good and Evil: Prelude to a Philosophy of the Future*, trans. Marion Faber (Oxford: Oxford University Press, 1998).

Paglia, Camille, *Sexual Personae: Art and Decadence from Nefertiti to Emily Dickinson* (New Haven, CT: Yale University Press, 2001).

Perreau-Saussine, Emile, *Catholicism and Democracy: An Essay in the History of Political Thought*, trans. Richard Rex (Princeton, NJ: Princeton University Press, 2012).

Ratzinger, Joseph, *Truth and Tolerance: Christian Belief and World Religions*, trans. Henry Taylor (San Francisco, CA: Ignatius, 2004).

Sheppard, Lancelot C., *Lacordaire: A Biographical Essay* (London: Catholic Book Club, 1964).

Index

agnosticism 64–6, 109
Angels, Fallen 55–7, 62–3, 67–9, 74, 90–1, 107, 111–18

comedy 2, 76–7, 79–80, 83–7, 89, 116

euthanasia 13–14, 16, 66, 71, 119

freedom 63–4
French revolution 47–8

idolatry 14–15, 19, 53, 110
integralism 62–3
Islam 9, 40, 64, 110

Lacordaire, Henri Dominique viii, 11, 47–53, 71, 105, 107, 109, 111, 119, 122
liberalism 11, 19, 62, 66

Nietzsche, Friedrich 55, 68, 79, 122

Prometheus 25–6, 37–8, 42–4, 55–7, 69, 73, 76, 89–90, 108–9, 111, 113–22
protestantism 33–6, 63

secular, secularity 6–7, 38–9, 47–51, 71, 73–7, 93–5, 99, 101–2, 121
secularism, secularization 8–11, 19, 32–3, 36, 41–2, 52, 61, 63, 73, 76–8, 81–3, 87, 95–8, 101, 105

time 31, 35–6, 41–2, 46, 49–51, 74–7, 80, 83, 93–5, 99, 103–4
tragedy 29, 76–7, 79–84, 86

Zeus 84, 90, 116

www.ingramcontent.com/pod-product-compliance
Lightning Source LLC
Chambersburg PA
CBHW070644300426
44111CB00013B/2248